A study of culture, belief and social structure
By

Tahir Iqbal © 2008

Dedicated to Bet
"if only you really knew,
if only I really knew,
what I'm going through,
I'd be with you"
(quote from Sonic Youth, Superstar)

Sponsored by:
www.maisonmascara.co.uk, maison mascara boutique b&b, 33 Montpelier road, Brighton, BN1 2LQ, UK.

TABLE OF CONTENTS

i) Introduction
ii) Idea Maps introduction
iii) Focal Points
iv) Feedback
v) lifeworlds and idea maps

0. The Logic of Truth, The Lie Paradox and The re-establishment of the Khalifah
1. Recovering economics from the theory
2. The role of falasafa (philosophy) in Economics
3. Counterfactuals in Life History Livelihood Studies of Poverty
4. Kaldor's Laws vs Keynes
5. Memetic house prices
6. Economic theorisation
7. Inflation and assets
8. Debt and Balance of Payments
9. On the dynamic system of the economy
10. On the nature of the economy
11. The world bank and poverty lines
12. Systems of thought
13. The production function
14. On the normal distribution
15. The theory of the Islamic state
16. Truth, Democracy and Statistics
17. A justification of a plan to end poverty through alternative Economic Theory
18. Perfect Competition, a critical disjuncture with the conventional wisdom
19. A Centre to a Circle
20. Anti-Americanism in British Society, The Universal Social Model and democracy
21. On Shafi'i
22. Causes of poverty, a short literature review
23. The nature of terrorism
24. The philosophical problem at the heart of dynamics of society
25. Non-reductionist Memetic Theory in relation to Habermas and Dawkins
26. The early 21st Century global circuits of trade and capital
27. The Private Equity model
28. Extensive form game theory applied to poverty and crime
29. What makes an idea successful?
30. Progressive social movements in the UK
31. Night Life (world)
32. On the salient characteristics of the underlying idea map of society
33. Integration of Muslims into the UK lifeworld?
34. The institutional determinants of trade
35. An Accumulation model
36. The limitations to growth in an unequal society

i) Introduction

The purpose of this collection of essays is to create a framework for interdisciplinary analysis of social science. This begins with philosophy, which we take to be considered examination of the most simple of issues and definitions, though we construct a narrative of one social science, economics, and discuss the problems and difficulties it faces in the strength of supposedly reasoned thinking within it. Principally we suggest that direct observation and reasoning from these real observations is the principal route to truth used by science. We argue that this is what interdisciplinary social science should observe. We propose that social science is concerned at its macro level with layers of interrelated processes which have their origins in history, institutions and social forces. A process is a sequence of connected events, which exists in the mind of the social scientist observer as an abstraction and is mapped from reality. The repetition of processes in history and across the world allows us to identify them, through seeing similar effects and similar structures we can deduce an abstract mechanism that is identified with the process. In addition our research strategy involves thinking about structures in reality and considering what the logic of these are, which allows us to do thought experiments aided by simulations in spreadsheets to allow us to isolate these processes' effects in asmuch as they are consistent phenomena. The reality that processes will lead to consistent effects at times is due to the existence of pervasive structures in society. The presence of a road will lead to a consistent flow of people going down it subject to certain conditions of population size and need for travel down that road. But structures do not necessarily have to be physical, a contract, such as a loan, with its concomitant features leads to various processes in society, indeed it has been considered by Minsky that the concept of the loan leads to our boom-bust economic cycle. Changing the structure of the loan in terms of who receives what and when would lead one to believe that different outcomes are possible. We have therefore some idea of how basic structures can be useful, insofar as one would like to eliminate recessions. One of our key points we find is that structures are often accepted, they are not dynamical optimising in the sense that they do not tend towards the best solution to society's problems necessarily. In the case of loans this is because the concept loan is determined historically and only changes in line with the whims and spirits of the banking industry, that is the complex that creates the loan. What should be noted is that a complex is also created of people who have borrowed money which itself creates the effects of boom-recession.

We discuss later the idea of a complex, the core of the process, the structure that causes the process to occur. When we look at the complexes later, we can get a handle on what is actually going on in the society and also appreciate that different outcomes can occur often with the same basic structure. Thus we a lead away from deterministic economic theory and into a realm whereby we can see risks to certain structures as well as appropriate ways of altering these outcomes. Our essays take us from seeing the world as being one of flux to rationalising why certain elements of society remain widely held and constant for long periods of time. An additional aspect of our analysis makes use of the concept of the 'scenario' (academically this is called the 'counterfactual'). This is taken from financial analysis used by industry practitioners in corporate finance in the City of London. A scenario approach involves looking at how the outcome of processes varies according to different events and environments, much as one might consider the variance of a population in addition to its mean. This does not mean that we look entirely at all possible events, in fact we are often most interested in the unlikely at any given time, yet possible and perhaps inevitable long term results of a process or system composed of processes. The essence of identification of a process is abstraction of mechanism, that is the focus on the observed driver of the dynamic in the object of enquiry. This is because we are looking for areas where the policy maker can cause change to the system, so what we can loosely call causal links found from abstraction of mechanism is important. This is not to side with the academic movement that seeks to find immutable, universal, ahistorical laws, as is the case in economics. Our judgement that society is the sum and interaction of many layers of processes within a context of free will, subject to tendencies yet not necessarily necessary ones.

We discuss a number of frameworks based on our methodology that springs from our criticisms of economic theory; debate structure and projected narrative, idea maps, conversation dynamics (both in terms of interaction as a game, e.g. through blocking strategies in conversation, and in terms of extensive form game theory as the multiple interaction of discussion), non-reductionist memetic-network lifeworld theory.

We apply these frameworks to several issues which are not all linked directly to economics, the area from where we started the discussion. These areas are the understanding of the tendency of poverty to lead to crime, the very structures of culture, the development of Islamic political theory, the understanding of Anti-Americanism as a social phenomena, the problem of analysing and solving poverty in the entire world, the issue of terrorism and several essays on aspects of economic theory; the core mechanism of the housing market, the aggregate production function and the debate on the source of economic growth, perfect competition. The wide variety of subject matter shows that this approach has the ability to make more ideas concerning many important issues.

From these frameworks we hope will grow research in social science from which we can be nearer to Truth and more helpful to the world which not only funds us but to which we owe a duty of care. Knowledge is about releasing the potential of humans.

ii) Idea Maps introduction

A key development and distinction in our analysis is the introduction and application of the 'idea map'. This requires further elucidation and the foundations of it must be made clear. Many things in society involve relationships, linkages, connections. As such any analytical tool must embody this. Relational analysis is a key part of Marxist theory in the social sciences. While critical theorists such as Adorno and poststructuralists, such as Barthes, acknowledged culture and developed narratives of this, we feel that a systematic technique is necessary for further development of the understanding of culture, particularly in modern post-industrial societies or indeed for any complex society that is the product of many different social forces. As an aside, this is a key tool in understanding multicultural societies, though the technique of 'idea maps' is not strictly restricted to ethnic groupings. Academic movements, debates, even individual essays can be brought into the rubric of idea maps. By creating an idea map we communicate complex social phenomena into a visual language, as Gaugin would have put it, directly accessible to the brain which then produces different information from the idea map that may shed light on issues that were previously opaque and intractable. If one puts a real life problem into mathematics, then one can reason using mathematical logic to create different information to the original observations. What we must make clear is that mathematics is not always suitable for understanding society since it has not developed the key complexity tools for analysing the social world. In addition mistakes made by economists in their abuse of mathematical reason can be understood as being similar to having an equation $x=y+1$ and then putting ones data on x and y into it in the incorrect variables to find the answer. Furthermore economists have also made the problem of arguing that the economy is, say, $x=y+1$, when in fact it is not possible as yet to put it into equations that have much in the way or meaning.

The foundation, the goal of idea maps is information compression. Just as a teacher will compress her judgement on the merit of a student's essay into a percentage number which relates to a class of a degree in order that the pupil will be able to adjust and improve their arguments, so idea maps are compression of information from some aspect of society that is based in ideas or can be represented as ideas. We use the unit of analysis as the idea, though this does not restrict the subdivision of ideas, loosely so that it can deal with complicated themes just as easily as individual arguments. The idea map can thus show the macro-picture (as would a lab microscope show a cell) or one can increase the level of detail to show a micro-picture (as an electron microscope would show much smaller surfaces of a biological sample). One can look at an idea map as similar in many ways to set theory, in the sense that it is essentially saying, what are the set of ideas that relate to a particular class of object of analysis. The new development in the framework is to draw links between one object and another relating to the sets of ideas that are contained within each object's 'idea set'.

An example of an idea map is the project of interdisciplinary social science. This is a grand project to bring together all social sciences away from division and produce multilayered narratives, theories and models to produce complete solutions and arguments drawn from all parts of social theory, sociology, economics, political theory, anthropology, human geography, history, etc. Consider part of the idea map produced by the project of interdisciplinary social science, that of methodological assumptions:

Sociology (homogeneity) – Anthropology (heterogeneity)
A part of the idea map of interdisciplinary social science

Here we can see the approach of connecting sociology which looks at the world to a far greater degree of homogeneity than anthropology. Thus we see a tension arising in the idea map. Clearly there is a degree of subjectivity to forming an idea map, just as one can focus on the eye in a Picasso painting or the mouth in it or perhaps the entire picture. A strong aversion to subjectivity in analysis may be considered by some to be unscientific, difficult to deal with. Yet two people can sit at a table and communicate that they both believe that a table exists that they are sitting at. While one may look at the legs of the table and the other looks at the surface, they may find agreement and should a third person come and disagree, there is the potential for the other two to obtain data and communicate this to the third party who may then become convinced. Above all this approach requires a certain level of intellectual maturity and focusing of the academic group involved in a debate concerning idea maps.

Idea maps can also be used to look at social groups, particularly, if one follows from Saussure, that language makes reality, thus social groups are the ideas attached to them. Consider the following idea map of Chinese social/political groups around the time of the Japanese occupation of China;

Kuomintang - Hatred of Japanese occupation - Communist party of China
    | |
Procapitalism   Anticapitalism/Communism

The above idea map shows the nationalist forces of the Government of China sharing a common idea with the Communist party under Mao of dislike of the Japanese occupation of parts of China. They thus entered into an alliance to fight and expel Japanese forces from China. However when the Japanese were removed, these two groups fought each other given that the mutually exclusive ideas of capitalism and communism brought in a tension among them. Clearly this does not do justice to a complete and compelling historical narrative that this period of history deserves, yet we can see that we can compress information such that clarity can be observed. Should someone disagree, they may bring forth their analysis which may show other facets of interest.

Mutual exclusivity is one of the perplexing questions involved in cultural analysis. This is where two ideas cannot both be held together since there is a strong tension among them. The above example of Capitalism or Communism, but it could be something more mundane as drink Pepsi/drink Coke. Clearly sometimes ideas synthesise, but there are often reasons due to their complete incompatibility that mean that this cannot occur. We will continue this particular discussion in our extension of the idea map methodology to memetic structural analysis where this question is most pertinent.

Values, that is the ideal ideas that form the basis for a nation-state, must be carefully analysed. By their nature they are 'models' rather than necessary action and thus reality. A nation may have the ideal value of freedom, yet may engage in reality against this. Very often much ideology can be divided into de facto and de jure, in the sense of what happens and what is understood to be good action. The reason for this division is that value is plausibly often an a posteori judgement of an action while the production of the action is not necessarily driven from a particular value. Care must also be taken to divide values as are propagated and values, such as greed, which are commonly held but do not, in many sections of society, hold much social reward for propagation. Values are a special case of an idea map and are sometimes related to political economy. An aspect of values is that they determine the moral high ground which different institutions and nation-states often strive to obtain, especially where there is conflict.

In summary, we argue that the idea map is a useful tool to simplify exposition and analysis of many facets of society, its institutions, history and knowledge. The key development is to identify the ideas related to an object of discussion and draw links with ideas from other objects of discussion. The links can be classed as being tensions, where ideas are non-coherent or in the extreme case, mutually exclusive. We hope that application of this information compression technique will elucidate many areas of society that have previously been opaque.

Idea maps have an internal process of change and development as well as an external one. This relates to a meta idea map which is often consensually held among participants of a society. An example which we discuss in modern society is the coherence rule, whereby ideas are added to the idea map in accordance with the principle that they are coherent with other ideas in the map. Liberalism leads to the end of slavery, while democracy tends towards direct democracy. As a thought experiment we can consider the effects of varying rules that determine the process of change of the idea map. So one could have a rule whereby the colour green was considered good. As a result ideas would become linked to the colour green, as is evident from the environmentalism social process impacting on company logos. Here we see that a fundamental and transcendental category in idea maps is the separation of good from evil. Perhaps one can say that this evolved from religion and has become a supreme way of categorising, debating and communicating different possible avenues of outcome and action. However the good of religion is in terms of altruism whereas the good of modern capitalism is in terms of benefit to the self. So we see that the transcendental categories are themselves idea maps. Idea maps are thus within idea maps within idea maps and so on.

This can be seen as the next step from Saussure's project of talking about reality in terms of language which he argued was a relational system. We see this to assume an intersubjective reality of signs that is potentially volatile yet obtains a paradoxical coherence and consistency across time. So instead of seeing reality as a system of related signs we see the social reality as being analysable through the schema of idea maps, the related system of ideas and their associations.

Clearly there is a neurobiological basis for this since ideas in the brain are supposed to be contained in neurons which are linked to others. Thus we obtain the idea of the subconscious whereby a racist sees the out group and associates negative characteristics to them. One may learn these links from existing publications and forms in the world, thus there is an element of this involved in the stability of idea maps. They must be stable to obtain a useful result in analysis. However people can write their own publications, communicate their own views, yet still there remains commonly held ideas and associations with other ideas. The possible reason why idea maps are stable is that there is a logical necessity to them, in as much as logic is used to produce and reproduce them. This logic is not necessary universal, different societies may have a different 'logic' or methodology for determining idea maps.

Yet we see that idea maps are intersubjective realities, they are formed like Habermas' lifeworlds in a consensual communicative set of acts among people involved with them. The prevalence of humanity to find itself meaning in domination is old as anything and the domination of ideas, since they make up our very consciousness, our very thoughts and thus our action, is self evident. This was Foucault's thesis.

iii) focal points

Essential to our work is the understanding of the idea of a focal point. This is an observation drawn from criticism by practitioners in industry, government and society that academic thought has a low level of applicability to their needs. If we define the service users of academic thought as a key consideration in the development of such debate and analysis then we see the need for understanding why academic thought does not cohere with the needs of practice. Since the practitioner is directly involved in influencing the system one may feel that their needs and concerns are more related to what is truth, while academics seek truth using reason. This is truly paradoxical.

Our argument for why this occurs is the difference in focal point of academic thought and the wider users of this thought in society. Academic thought as it exists today is a complex idea map involving Liberalism, Scientific method, The definition of individual ownership of ideas, a privileging of objectivity and systematic analysis, reason and logic. Each individual academic subject has different additional consensual idea maps that define the subject itself. Deviation from this underlying idea map is socially controlled by members of the group by means of disciplinary control systems, such as the fear of loss of status or respectability. This is not always the case, revolutionising the underlying idea map can also result in the academic being ascribed as a genius. It is argued that idea maps which are consensually held have an impact on the development of new ideas. From Velleman, the subject's need for coherence is a key process in the development of thought. Thus where the underlying idea map of an academic debate is consensually held there is a drive to make all new ideas 'fit in' to this base idea map. Since the underlying idea map is the overlapping set of methodological ideas and world views of the subject it generates a tendency to condition any new ideas in the subject. The reality faced by Foucault that the very terms of our language and implicitly the arguments involved in the underlying idea maps are historically generated by many factors that have little to do with the subject matter, such as political economy, particularly strategies employed by social groups for their goals, or historical incidents, such as the great focus on cutting inflation after the 1970s leading to theories that had at the core of the analysis the linking of inflation to money supply. The thing to notice here is that the theories focused on a specific area, a focal point.

Consider a Picasso painting. One can look at the eye, the nose, the face or the entire painting as it is. What we say about the painting depends on what we focus on, our focal point. Thus the data collected for empirical analysis and even the very creation of theories, depends on our focal point.

We suggest that the mechanism of coherency in a subjects idea map diverts the path of debate in respect of shared focal points. A focal point is often determined by the character of the academic, the underlying idea map and the path of the debate. A focal point is thus not something that will adhere to the truth. One can see a common Gestaltian picture of two faces that look like a vase depending on what one focuses on. Thus the same data can imply different 'truths' or at least varying arguments. Even the issue of what data is collected and what constitutes the unit of analysis can vary with focal points. Look at the EU, Britain, Scotland, Glasgow and a family living in Glasgow.

In our opening essay we suggest that economic theory has the incorrect focal point because it is subject to the dynamics of debate we have discussed, particularly in respect of being moulded and distorted by intervention of political economic social forces. In this way we choose to alter the underlying idea map involved in economic theory, that we say is called 'rigorous analysis' and instead privilege the focal point of the questions that society faces as givens. Whilst economic theory seeks to find a justification to what society should do in terms of 'rigorous analysis' and rejects the objectives and goals that come from society, it creates a weak social force that is in line with ideological concerns. We argue here that practitioners need to know what can be done, what options they have and what concomitant risks are implied to each option. This is an alternative scheme for the debate to structure itself around, maybe a methodology or perhaps more likely an ethos. This imposes a tendency on debate and empirical and logical theorisation to obtain results that are non-prescriptive but allow interest groups of many colours to have a central form of communicating their arguments.

We suggest future research in methodology could involve looking at how methodological rules (both implicit and explicit) determine the kind of knowledge created and the dynamic path it involves. Were a criteria for truth known then the outcome of methodological rules could be compared in respect of the truth. For example, one could be exclusively deductive, yet because the tools one has that are considered deductive are simple and do not adhere to the real processes in the object of study, one can see that one will constantly be leaving reality with ones knowledge. An example of this is the use and abuse of mathematics in economic theory, which has found itself impinging on other social sciences.

iv) Feedback

A crucial development in thinking occurred in the 'Cambridge Debate' on the coherency of the underlying idea map of laissez faire economics with Sraffra's introduction of feedback between variables, particularly capital and its price. The key point we take from this is that economic systems, and indeed cultural and belief systems, involve the flow of variables passing through each one many times. Thus water is brought to the sea by the river and then evaporates into the atmosphere to return to the river in the form of rain. What should be noted is the core mechanism of unidirectional complex systems which we analysed through a series of matrices in a spreadsheet and found that where the movement of a unit of, say, money flows from one agent to another in one direction, there is, irrespective of the size of the entire network, a common dynamic which can be represented as a triangular network of 3 agents each passing on either an ever increasing amount of a substance, a stable quantity or a decreasing amount. This can be represented as an equation of transference between agents x,y,z of $f(x(t))+x(t-1)=f(y(t-1))+y(t-2)=f(z(t-2))+z(t-3)$, where agents are assumed to transfer the quantity by an equal proportion by the function $f(\ )$. Should $df(\ )/dt$ be positive, in other words if an increasing amount is transferred each time, then the system tends towards an increasing, perhaps exponential amount of increase. There is thus hysteria or apathy. Boom or bust. Hate or Love. Understanding complexity and the varying indeterminate dynamics it presents opens a new era in social science. The simplifying analysis of social science has difficulty in giving prescriptions for the varying strategies an actor can involve themselves in to alter the social system, whether they are a radical revolutionary or a conservative capitalist.

We integrate the observations of the implication of feedback into our analysis. Particularly we talk about the total level of loans being a function of asset value due to the institution of the banking sector. A second area is the production of hate between different cultures and social groups. A third area where feedback is involved is in the structural dependencies of the poor in terms of environment, strategy and will. We argue that poverty leads to crime through the feedback in the system that a poor person experiences, in terms of their lifeworlds interacting to cause frustration and thus negatively associated behaviour and strategy.

The understanding of complex systems (a complex system is where there are many components that cannot be summarised in terms of the core mechanism of causal effects which often have properties of the system as a whole (emergent effects) distinguishable and indeed not clearly from any individual component) must be developed in social science as it is the very frontier of knowledge at present. Physics understands that

Newton gives no predictions for the 'many body problem', the complex systems of this subject. We give the option for developing our understanding of complexity through simulation of systems in spreadsheets where there is a numerical aspect or in terms of the rational imagination where there is a more subjective idea involved. We do use mathematical ideas, yet avoid some of the traps and blind alleys of conventional economic theory by interpreting simple findings about structures that occur in economies sometimes which we can actually see. This may seem an obvious point, yet no economist has been able to jump out of the constraints of the debate in economics which has lead economists down a path of unsophisticated simplicity of equations. The maths used by economists has been too simple yet too complex to understand. It has not understood that there are many very simple facts about the economy, simple structures that repeatedly appear, as well as complex emergent properties. The fact is we need new mathematics bespokely designed for complex systems such as economies and sophistication in our insight and clarity in our mapping of phenomena to our models. We find in our analysis that many problems such as financial and economic crises could have been understood better with such an approach.

v) lifeworlds and idea maps

Habermas in his Theory of Communicative Action discusses the concept of the 'lifeworld'. We can summarise this idea as a division of society into a set of interpersonally derived consensus' which have a goal or reason adduced by the members of the lifeworld. The lifeworld can be seen much like an idea map at varying levels of magnification, a lifeworld is composed of many lifeworlds which are themselves composed of many more. This concept is primarily used by Habermas to contradict the functionalist sociology of Mead and Parsons which sought to draw an analogy between society and the organ analysis of a biological being. In the sense that a lifeworld is a linguistic extensive form game theoretic state of existence for people. Since the lifeworld is the common existence of humans, then the process of developing this into a world as the functionalists would have us believe society was is less clear.

Habermas talks of lifeworlds being divided in keeping with Durkheim's belief that capitalism divided and alienated through anomie social relations. We discuss later the common phenomena of 'nightlife' in Western capitalism, whereby social relations divided by work (the division of labour) become reunited and form complex transient networks in the experience of the lifeworld of 'going out on the town', that is leisure activities after work with friends particularly going to nightclubs and pubs. Therefore, in terms of time geography, Western capitalism finds its legitimacy, production and reproduction in the weekly cycle of work and nightlife.

We see the lifeworld as a loose term for a social element of intersubjective consciousness, where there are rules, norms, systems of domination (both in terms of individuals in hierarchy and in terms of idea maps of the very meaning of the lifeworld and its components, as well as and the interpretative dialogue which can be summarised by conversation trees), actions and consequences.

So work is a lifeworld from the standpoint of the actors involved in the theatre of work. Play is a lifeworld for children, while nightlife is the adult analogue. The interconnections between these two in the formation and reproduction of nightlife is self evident. A holiday is an experience of a lifeworld that is of another culture and society to some extent or perhaps a hybrid of ones own culture of leisure and another's.

What should be clear is that an individual may have many lifeworlds, indeed they may even occur at the same time, as is the case with networking, where a businessperson socialises for the purpose of making new business contacts. Another example is religion, a British Muslim may have the lifeworld of Islam while at the same time follow the lifeworld of influencing the state, engaging in politics. The lifeworld of Islam involves a cycle of activity involving prayer, charity giving, fasting, engaging in the defence of other Muslims among other prescriptions. A Muslim who is at work will often go to prayer at the specified times. Thus the two lifeworlds are held simultaneously.

The Islamic lifeworld is generated, as we will discuss further below, by a social organisation of Islamic scholars, the criteria of that being a matter of debate, who create what can be analysed as an idea map, where action is divided into, for example, obligatory or wajb (like prayer), good but not obligatory (such as helping a poor person beyond ones basic charity obligations), disliked acts, etc. We discuss further that the evolution of this Islamic idea map has involved a kind of coherence process with new kinds of actions being added to this categorisation as defined by scholars who themselves follow a certain analytical method. Thus the Islamic idea map is a interconnection of lifeworlds whereby scholars debate with an existing idea map of previous scholarly doctrines (normally seen as the main schools of accepted Islamic thought) that forms an idea map in the mind and social group of various Muslims that is then the producer of the lifeworld of the Muslim in terms of their religion.

Thus we see that idea maps and lifeworlds form systems which can be the analytical basis for further research of connected case studies into a variety of social objects of enquiry.

0. The Logic of Truth, The Lie Paradox and The re-establishment of the Khalifah

The Logic of Truth

Ibn Taymiyyah introduced the proposition that the internal mental state does not cohere necessarily with the external state of the world. People can be wrong in other words. Consider probability, inflation, and more broadly; models and theories. These even though they may be produced from logical deductions and empirical evidence are ideas imposed on the world. True the world may be logical and work in the same method as the mind, but it is an inductive argument to suggest that deductively produced theories work consistently. And inductive arguments are not necessary truth. The chicken may see the farmer feed it every day yet one day it will see a knife at its throat.

Consider for example the process involved in creating a theory. A set of facts lead one to a reorganisation of information into an idea, such as probability, which is then applied to other circumstances and transformed back into a prediction. Consider a parallel case of information encoded, then transmitted to someone else who does not have the key to unscramble the code. The decoding of the message cannot necessarily occur except by chance to reform as the original message. Thus we may be allowed doubt in respect of an idealisation of reality, perhaps a rearrangement of reality such as probability, that is used to take facts and produce causal laws that have relevance in many areas. Even if the theory is applied to the very same subject matter that it originally issues from, then we are unsure if any facts can necessarily be supposed to be deduced from the idealisation's rule based process.

The means to avoid such pitfalls are to carefully cohere every element of the logic, rules, syntax and data to the external object in question. This is important in both the process of production of knowledge from facts as it is in the translation both ways from reality to theory to reality back again. This follows from our analogy with the encoded message. The message must be consistently encoded and decoded to retain its integrity.

Should this be the key to knowledge, perhaps an implicit rule followed in successful sciences, then the question becomes what are the rules to guide the appropriate coherence, coding and decoding of the data? Clearly the first issue is a certain element of desire for the truth to be the outcome of knowledge. Before action comes hope. Secondly critical examination of the idealisation to justify itself in terms of its coherence with reality are important. Thirdly, the collection of evidence to underlie the coherence of idealisation to reality. Fourthly corroboration and elaboration of each element of the argument put forward by the theory is vital. Elucidation and transparency of every step, implicit or otherwise must be undertaken.

Can one provide an analytical proof that such method leads to mental belief cohering with reality. We call this the 'Logic of Truth'. The external reality is represented as (I) set of information. I is converted by the idealisation by the function f(.) to an idealised external reality which is the theory- T. $f(I) => T$. The theory leads to deductions the results of which are a function t(.). Thus $f(I) => T$, $t(T)$ therefore $t(f(I))$. The results t(T) are then translated back to external reality in the form of beliefs about causality, understanding of processes, in other words implications of the theory. The implications of t(T) are a mapping of theory to reality given by m(.). Thus the process of creating knowledge is $t(f(I)) => m$. If an untrue element occurs in this process then the mapping m to reality will result in what could be false knowledge. 'm' is a subset of the original reality I, given that m is true. If m is not true because any element in the aforementioned process is misleading or false then m will be false thus it cannot be part of the original reality I, thus the process leads to a contradiction and is thus false. Thus each step must be truthful in this conversion of fact into theory into implications. We feel that this careful approach has been overlooked by science and social scientists leading to less tenable theories and policy. We feel that a debate starting from our 5 rules of the methodology to obtain truth, justified by our analysis on the logic of truth, can be a starting point to new and better science.

Many idealisations such as probability do not exist in reality in the sense that one can objectively identify them, but their effects can be seen. This would be the instrumentalist approach to knowledge. If the effects or predictions of these idealisations can cohere with reality then there is a credible belief that the theory that makes them is useful. It may be that the theory represents a dominant process in reality that is not contingent on any other factors that are ignored in the analysis. In such a scenario we can agree with the instrumentalist and refine our definition of the process of creation of truth (m). That is to say that I may be a combination of two sets; I' and I* where the former is the dominant causal information in reality and I* is the non-causal information in reality. In such a case this special case of instrumentalist reason is simply a substitution of I with I' where I* is ignored in the analysis. Clearly even one case of I*'s information affecting the outcome on m would undermine the logic of truth we have developed. If the utility of the instrumentalist based theory is in its predictions then a misalignment between prediction and reality would lead to a decline in its utility.

There is the special case also of when reality, I, works under the same rules and processes of logic. This is the position held in much of science. Thus a deduced proposition is held to predict reality. We feel that such a position requires a proof, yet it is something that is often felt to be held unconditionally, which is by definition unjustified. We have argued above that for reason to work we must work with reason. That is to say that the logic of truth is something to be analysed and elucidated to produce a debate on the appropriate methodological rules for understanding different systems of reality.

Thus we come back to Ibn Taymiyyah's insight that the internal reality is not necessarily coherent with the external reality. However, rather than rejecting reason we believe it is possible to guide reason out of the maze it finds itself in through debating methodology.

Self-referentiality- The Lie Paradox analysed and implications for the rules of the logic of truth.

What I am saying now is a lie. This statement is the well known Lie Paradox which is simultaneously true and false at the same time. An idea map analysis of this is;

Coherence of statement to definition of a true statement i.e. the statement is Truth (given statement is false) - Statement - False (given belief that the statement is true)

The disaggregation of the statement into its compositional ideas sheds light on this longstanding puzzle. The paradox leads to two different statements which are associated with it and are confused together as being truth. Truth is coherence of a statement to the definition of a true statement but it is also considered belief that is true given the information we have. Coherence of a statement to truth and belief that necessitates truth are thus two different kinds of truth that do not have to be considered the same thing.

There are many ideas such as the self-fulfilling prophecy where belief necessitates truth. This is where the external reality is determined by belief. Clearly there are many outcomes depending on the distribution of belief in one or other course. A run on a bank, caused by a belief (founded or unfounded) that a bank is insolvent, is an example of the self-fulfilling prophecy. A belief in oneself, confidence to overcome any challenge, will likely be found as a characteristic of many successful people. They believe they can succeed thus they do succeed, contingent on a number of other factors. The truth that is the internal reality is something that creates indeed is a causal factor in external reality. It is a different thing to the coherence of statement and truth though, in the sense that the statement is not active, it is not an actor in the system. Without the belief the truth of the outcome of the belief may not occur. This is different to a coherence of statement to truth in that without the statement the truth would potentially still be true though clearly if nobody had thought of the statement then this truth would simply not be something known.

A coherence between a statement and the definition of truth is defined as the internal reality (mental state) of the acceptance of the statement is linked in identity to the external reality. The definition of truth inasmuch as it refers to an external reality is often held to be something that can be disassembled and joined together. Thus the work of knowledge. It seems to be a reasonable belief that truth that coheres with the external reality is joinable to other truths to produce, through logical rules, new truths. Yet there is the possibility of a logical dynamic at variance with the external reality, perhaps even when we have full information. Consider a system that has a dynamic that is not known to logic. In the absence of knowledge of the system's dynamics the rules of logic can be applied to the subject matter but will not find useful information, just as solving the equation $x+y=1$ with only the knowledge of that equation will not tell you the hidden information; x and y.

Indeed consider $x+y=1$. If we know y then we can solve for x. Consider the idea map involved in this. Information involved in specification of the problem is that y is given, while there is also a relation whereby when y is higher, x is lower, and vice versa and this is given by the condition that $x+y=1$. The archetypal technique in mathematics of obtaining information from having data and relational information is clearly something of truth. Here the result of the technique of mathematics along with the setup of the problem is a statement that coheres with the truth. The internal reality is however not related to the external reality. One cannot actually find many equations in reality that are exactly the same as the many equations one can write down. Since one can write an infinite amount of equations given enough time, an assumed spatially finite universe cannot hold all things that can be represented as all equations that can be written down. This argument would seem to undermine our earlier contention of the logic of truth requiring analogous relations between the idealisation process and the dominant part of the external reality in question. However, an equation can be constructed and a representation of it can be put into reality, assuming that the equation is logically consistent and valid, thus there is no finite universe problem in the analysis of the logic of truth. The second counterargument to the logic of truth is that mathematical equations such as $x+y=1$ can allow truthful deductions. For those who believe our argument for the logic of truth implies that such deductions are false or unreliable, I would say that such an interpretation is too strict and perhaps misleading, since though one may have difficulty in finding $x+y=1$ in reality, one could reasonably be expected to be able to represent it in reality. Indeed many mathematics school teachers make a living from doing just that. This allows us to seek coherence with scepticism of knowledge and logical deductions. If the logical deduction can be represented in reality then the logical deduction coheres necessarily with reality, given the trivial fact that a representation is correspondence.

There is thus a clarification necessary of our rules for the logic of truth. The correspondence of the idealisation to reality must be considered in a broader sense whereby the mind is not removed from reality. If an idealisation can be represented in reality through the action brought about by the mind then the theory does cohere with that representation that is created by the mind. Thus we see a much more nuanced and developed formulation of the deep philosophy of knowledge first considered by Ibn Taymiyyah.

The implications for the determination of the objectives of Shariah from the Logic of Truth

The argument put forward by the Ulema (scholars) of Islam is that the Shariah has the objective of following God's law. This is said to be given in the Holy Texts and History of the Prophet. Shafi'I is known to have supported the use of analogy in other words generalisation of Islamic rules from scripture and action of the messenger to areas not directly covered by those rules. The assumption here is that Allah (SWT) must have compressed or encoded His rules that can be uncompressed through the application of analogical thought by a select group of scholars.

We wish to analyse this in a coherent and truthful manner. In this regard we must follow the best understanding we can have in our opinion and knowledge. To do less would risk criticism from Allah (SWT) just as a child who disregards their better knowledge is scolded by their parents with the statement 'you know better than this to do that wrong thing'.

The reality we are trying to determine here is God's desire for the constitution of human action. This is a broader and more inclusive definition than many Ulema's objectives since they seek to determine logically the laws of mankind rather than the full and complete set of action that constitutes God's wants for humanity. True many scholars decide on preferred actions, good actions, as well as bad actions which one normally feels of law. However, Islam is seen to be a complete religion, thus they do not go far enough in discussion of the generality and fundamental process and truth of the world of action, in other words by determining the law rather than its spirit, meaning and reasoning.

What is also overlooked by the scholarly debates is the relation between the competence for good action and the following of God's wishes for human action. Developing the capabilities for good action are as important as good action. Thus this discussion which seeks to objectively enhance and clarify the wants of God is crucial since by understanding God's message better we have a greater capacity to do good action.

Following the Logic of Truth, we take God's wishes and turn them into an idealisation, reason from this idealisation to produce a mapping onto classification of action, steps necessary to build capability for achieving such action and enhancement of competence in continuing the development of good action.

We can not hear God, though we can use the scripture as a model to determine what God might suggest on differing subjects and contingencies. This is exactly what most Ulema do at present. The more difficult question is what form does the idealisation of the model of God's wishes take? You may quote Ibn Taymiyyah and suggest that no idealisation is necessary. But even a literal reading, in other words a one to one mapping of scriptural rule to law to action is an idealisation. Even law 'a' leads to action 'a' is an idealisation, albeit a simple and straightforward one. $1=1$ is an equation. Since we are not all-knowing, we cannot assert the superiority of one or other idealisation without consideration of the implications, relative value and consistency of the alternative possibilities. Even Ibn Taymiyyah produced justification, considered and elegant, of his views.

Every Muslim who prays wishes 'Rabbna ar-tinna fi-douniar hasanna, wa fil akhira-ti hasanna'; 'our Lord, gives us the good in *this life* and in the *next life*". Thus there is perhaps a wish made by all Muslims who pray to seek good in this life as well as the next. A judgement of action must thus be seen in relation to its effect in this life and in the next. The fact of one's fate in the next life being contingent on doing 'amali salihati' (good deeds- external faith) as well as on 'amanu' (belief and faith- internal faith) is repeated many times in the Quran. Thus from these statements we can suggest that the objective of Shariah is to raise the competence, capability and realised action of doing good deeds. Note that there is no where in the Quran stated that there is a limit to doing good. It can be seen as an extension of Zakat and Sadaquah (charity), for the Prophet (SWL) has said that 'Smiling is charity', thus we can see that anything that helps another apart from oneself is charity, though one's intentions should align with the good action. Good must be seen in the context of outcome in this life as well as the next. Thus we see that the broad objective of Shariah is the improvement of the lot of all people in this life and the next.

The problematic now becomes how does one determine the best course of action, the identification of good deeds and determine the development of capability to do good deeds by enhancing one's ability to identify what is good.

The answer is given in the Quran. The determination of the good must be the Khalifah, the decision maker of Muslims. But who should be Khalifah? Since no one is all-knowing individually this becomes a complicated choice. However, were all Muslims throughout the world to be as one complex, in a perpetual debate that strove towards consensus through rational, careful, objective, respectful discussion, then would that body, the Ummah, be the best qualified? Inasmuch as one can develop a powerful computational result from many computers working together, can not an Ummah brought together by the desire to understand what it truly means to be good, to find new ways of being good, to progress and provide for the needs of humanity, be closer to all-knowing than complete ignorance? Thus we call for the re-establishment of the Khalifah, but in a form that unites all muslims, irrespective of their initial positions. Instead of Allah's representative being an individual, it would instead become every Muslim engaged in debate with every other Muslim. Allah has said that division of the Muslim people is wrong, so this policy which unites Muslims is perhaps a commendable thing.

1. Recovering economics from the theory

There is a fact most policy makers and some economists know. This is that economics is essentially lies. This thesis is to be proved in this essay. In addition we consider an appropriate philosophical redirection of the debate in economic theory. We outline the reasons why debate in economics has moved so far from Truth which is our basis for explaining and justifying the strategy to make economics a subject of science rather than ideology.

Economics takes a methodology of science and looks for causal laws, structures that produce stable results. This leads to a desire to measure and evaluate through statistical analysis. We believe this most fundamental of approaches is wrong. The biggest problem with this is that human's have free will. To assume stability in such a system is fraught with overconfidence in the analytical approach of economics. To assume that there may be a stability of effects and cause produced by the structure of society, i.e. norms, values and institutions, that is historically contingent, is deftly put away with the sociological argument that losers from such a social structure can change the structural aspects of society to make themselves winners, thus the social structure is not an equilibrium. We would perhaps be lead to the belief that all is flux, ever changing randomness, in respect of the outcome for society. Yet we only begin at this stage.

The core of economics is to advise the policy maker in a nation-state and of international organisations. The result economics must produce is the development of structures that aid the accumulation of the world. The insight we bring to the debate is that the policy maker does not need to know the exact effect and relations of various policy instruments. It does not need to know every detail of the future path of GDP or any other statistic. It just needs to know what is the best policy and what is the solution to various problems thrown up by events. Thus the exacting analysis of economics can be discarded. Rigour in logical argument needs replacing with rigour in observation and making the focus point involve the concerns of different societies in their own set of underlying consensual idea maps.

Economic theory has developed along a line of ever greater complexity of mathematical artifacts that lead to one conclusion. That the best answer is some concept called the "market" and there is nothing that can be done to improve on this. Clearly this is an ideological result that weakens the case for debt-orientated trade capitalism for society which sees through the lies and reduces the ability of the state to effectively dig capitalism out of the holes it finds itself in at many junctures in history. We suggest that if policy makers had a greater insight into the economy and the social sphere, then accumulation could be much higher and more sustained. If you understand how a machine works in Truth then you are more likely to be able to fix it when it is broken. If we don't fix it then we will be broke.

Thus in terms of maintaining the development of capitalism we argue that long term accumulation needs an eye above the system. An eye that sees through lies and brings better results. The vacuity in explaining the effect of the market without delving into the ever changing structures built by markets is evident. The economist may say that they are simplifying, yet few know anything about what it is to do business. Few business people know what others are doing in the economy and more pertinently, how this all fits together. The question is often left unanswered as to whether a political-economic-social structure tends towards growth and the assessment of risks of different structures. Adam Smith developed his ideas from observation of the economy. He draws the example of the pin that is produced through separate specialised processes and uses this observation to focus his analysis on the economy. He identifies a process in reality and then considers the implications of this. We hope to bring economists back to the basic technique of Adam Smith.

Economists have since Smith developed reasoning from truths. A person may be assumed to optimise for themselves. Therefore they may do the best thing for themselves. Therefore they are always allocating at best. Errant economists from the centre and left have criticised economic theory by falling into a trap of working within that system of thought. Williamson says the perfect market is efficient yet it is transactions costs which lead the outcome away from optimality. The point is that true reasoning, where the assumption and logic are truth, does not necessarily confer with reality. The fact is that science begins and ends with observation. To observe the sun in motion from the Earth we would happily believe that it is the earth that is stationary until observation shows that this is incorrect. But deeper than this, one can prove with argument contradictory points simply by changing the terms of the structure of the system one is observing. In other words we need to accurately define what it is that we are dealing with to avoid misleading logical conclusions.

What we suggest is that the social world is a collection of processes. These processes are connected sequences of events that have effects on various objects of interest. They exist in the sense that they can be identified and observed though sometimes they are only present in effect. Economic theory is in fact hypothetical processes that may or may not exist. The process of the perfect market producing the lowest cost may be true. The consumer who is optimising between two choices may be happy. Though, of course, the history of revolutionary activity would suggest to the contrary. Economics has generated many hypothetical analytical instruments that have a coherence due to being attached to mathematic results, but we argue that this mapping of mathematical structures to the material reality is naïve to the point of being deceptive. For example an equation is set of the average person's choice to obtain happiness through either allocating their endowment of time to either work or leisure. Reality ends here though in the economist's analysis as the person is then analysed in terms of optimising a function of their happiness where the control variables are 'solved' in mathematics of dynamic optimisation (from Bellman's technique) whereby each time period's equations are optimised. The circularity of the logic, that the person is assumed to always try to optimise to their own benefit and thus the results of an optimising process such as; dynamic optimisation, lagrangian analysis, optimal control theory, lead to a result that is in line with what economists want to say, that is that the market left unhindered always produces the best results. The idea map here is a connection of;

greed – person optimises – mathematical optimisation tool – economic interpretation

We suggest that the final element in the argument of the economist, that the mathematical result of an optimisation tool is linkable in truth to economic results is unsound. A simple reason why this is the case is that the mathematical tool does not exist in reality, one cannot find indifference curves or pontangryin's maxima principle in the world. Thus we see that the onus is on economists to show that these things actually exist before jumping to their naïve conclusions. A second reason why the economist is lead astray is that the process involved in mathematical optimisation do not map onto real processes, no one actually solves an equation to choose what to buy or could be seen to be doing a similar process in abstraction. The third reason is that the assumption of optimality of the agent necessitates the optimality of the result, thus the assumption is the cause of the answer and the mathematics is obfuscation. The existence of social processes, whereby there are features of the whole of society that are not necessarily evident in any particular individual, lead one to see that there may be things that cannot be readily put into mathematics. The fact that the individual is a part of a greater whole, one that has a historical contingency and is defined by an interaction of individual with the society, leads one to realise that more work is needed on the very basics of who we are and what we do both in terms of ourselves, our identities, our national and international realities, before we can formalise results in mathematics. Indeed looking at most mathematics used in economics, we see that the most important aspects of the reality, such as accumulation and the flow of money from one person to another, are not easily mapped into calculus. The reason why is that calculus has results for simple equations that one finds in physics, where the system is compressed into causal laws, one variable being determined by another. However, an economy is centrally about a network of flows determined by capabilities, contracts, intersubjective realities (idea maps) and the level of accumulation (which is determined by the level of surplus flow) among other things. We argue later that simulation of networks of people in a spreadsheet can give important results in terms of how the relative power of people to extract money from others is set up. This also has emergent properties that would not immediately be clear, for example we show that an unequal network can tend towards stagnation.

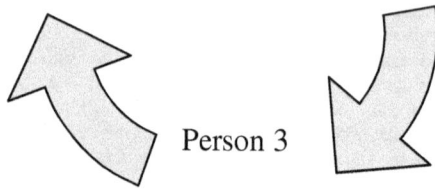

The diagram above shows a simplification of people giving money to one another (given by the direction of the arrows) where person 1 gives money to person 2 who gives money to person 3 who then gives to person 1 again, and so on. In the presence of feedback in the system (where everyone buys goods from each other) we believe that there is this central abstract mechanism at work. Formulation of a network of people who give money to each other by way of a transformation matrix which gives the percentage of money that each person gives to each other in the elements of the matrix leads one to confirm that this structure is likely to be a realistic mapping of model to reality. This system can be considered as a iterative map:

$Y(3) = aY(2) = aY(1)$: time=1

Where $Y(x)$ is the income of the xth person in the network and a is an assumed equal proportion of income that is given to the next person. If a is greater than 1, in other words more money is given each time than the initial income then there is an ever increasing tendency to the network. Such an example is where there is debt allowed in the system, whereby a person spends more than their income by borrowing. Where a is less than 1, i.e. where there is saving, then this economy eventual grinds to a halt as less and less money is transferred each time.

Putting $Y(3)$ in terms of $Y(1)$ we see the simple result:

$Y(3) = a^2 Y(1)$

Thus as time passes the rate of increase of the system where a is greater than 1 is increasing (since the derivative of the equation is greater than 1). Thus this system has a tendency to boom because of feedback. In the presence of debt there comes a time in the economic cycle where the debt repayments come to reduce the value of a, thus the system then suffers falls in money flow, thus a recession.

Economists have long accepted that their analysis is not perfectly real, but their most common refrain is that this is because there is nothing better to replace it with. Here we see that we can certainly find insight from developing analysis of real mechanisms that are generated from the pervasive structures of the reality. If we get the structure correct, both in terms of mapping reality into abstraction and then mapping abstraction back to reality, then we see from this example that there is a realistic hope that such a research strategy could be fruitful. We do however, need to develop the basic research, the conceptual categories that we define to allow us to talk. Without language one cannot discuss reality.

We need to talk about the structure that generates processes to understand where to begin in our analysis. A complex is a set of interacting agents in a system which gives rise to processes though not exclusively. No individual agent has control of the results of the complex, they may even know these effects, they may even suffer because of it. Yet they hold to it as if they were imprisoned in structure. This is not to say that there can be no change to this structure, it is simply that the bonds of the complex are widely held and the ability to bring change to the complex is difficult, perhaps because there are so many people in it or perhaps because people who reject the complex lose their ability to affect the structure. We muse later on the cause of consensus, which we believe is in some ways a desire for coherence among equal people, so that once a structure exists it may not necessarily lead to change of itself even when its members are not completely at peace with it. This is not to exclude other explanations, for example the memetic property of humanity, that is that people simple copy others, or the learning aspect, whereby people are socialised by education and family power structures into having a coherent intersubjective reality.

Foucault argued that the world was the result of historical structures such as prisons, psychiatric hospitals and the intellectual complex of psychology, the state, that created the very terms of words that form our consciousness both individual and social. From these examples we can hypothesise that processes have an impact on language and therefore thought in addition to the relations and organisation of humanity. Language needs more systematic analysis in terms of its structure of interaction as well as in the dynamic process of convincing someone and altering of opinion involved in transferral of a message from one person to another.

But in terms of economics, we must see that processes also have material impacts. The process of hypercapitalism, whereby banks find ever smaller numbers of low risk individuals to lend to yet need to continue the cycle of credit and deposits weaken their prudence in lending and therefore less financial sophisticated people become heavily indebted. The process of property speculation leads to people only selling their house if they make an acceptable return. Thus there is continual house price rises. A complex of social relations leads to this house price rise becoming seemingly cemented into the public psyche. Inflation is a similar complex of wage bargaining institutions, government and business.

In respect of policy creation, one can analyse complexes and their resultant processes and effects on policy objectives. Coupling processes together, perhaps through the creation of complexes can be used to influence material results for the economy and indeed for social policy.

Marx can be understood not for his contribution to truth but rather for the process he created using the then nascent free working class. By latching onto a current and logic of liberalism, that is of equality, and bringing it to the fore of his belief that this should be an economic equality, brought the interests of the working class against those of capitalism. This lead to the development of a conflict in society. The essence of progress is that the logical extension of a belief are the next step in action. We assert that change is often in the direction of consistency and coherency. The idea of progress is that there must be change. Consider the similarity with Islamic theology where the process is to create further extensions of sacred rules to new areas using the original directions though clearly without much discussion on the spirit of the law. Here the motion of change is determined by the structure meta-narrative and resultant institutions of Ulema (Islamic theologians) based on the ideas of Shafi'i.

A key social process for development of non-industrial countries involves the creation of a working class and an accumulating capitalist class. We must see that in many LDCs (Less Developed Countries) the migration of agricultural farmers to cities has resulted in some cases in the enlargement of a working class. Examples include Pakistan and China in recent years. The key to capitalist development is the existence of these basic classes as social groups, which springs from idea maps of these groups and social structure that defines, reproduces and maintains these groups as real things. The capitalist class needs to have an accumulatory or covetous idea of being (that is how they see themselves as an objective or a rule of maximisation of saving). The working class often needs to be a consumer of capitalist goods and therefore an essential point needed for accumulation of the capitalist class is for there to be a market for production, which the working class provide in part. We see that once the insertion of the idea of capitalism and the necessary institutional structures of it are in place then the process of production, accumulation, consumption can begin to draw in non-capitalist classes into the system. A hypothesis of Africa's lost decades of development is that this matrix of institutions, the capitalist class, the working class, and the value adding processes of the firm (in terms of technology, social organisation, markets and marketing, business strategy, the lack of government intervention into the 'beliefworld' of the society) has not been tackled coherently by actors including government.

What we see here in abstract terms is that ideas and social structures (such as rules, strategies, beliefs, essentially idea maps, lifeworlds and the synthesis of these two- the 'beliefworld) can create and alter social processes. This general policy point must be fully internalised for the practitioner to obtain the most benefit from these essays.

2. The role of falasafa (philosophy) in Economics

Many economists ascribe a key role to theory for informing and structuring theoretical developments in the literature. Without theory one would not know what data to collect and how to put this together. Yet where does theory start? We suggest that the impatience to produce results leads economists away from Truth, the true system that is present in reality. The essential seed of knowledge is philosophy (falasafa), the first academic subject. Going back to the roots of knowledge in order to better avail oneself to the Truth is we argue, essential.

The argument is stated that we need to ground our analytical work in reality, as objectively as we can. If we do not begin in reality, although we may end up in theoretical constructs, we can have a hunch that we may never be near to the truth. The story of people with blindfolds; one who felt the trunk of an elephant and decided it was a rope, another who felt the leg and decided it was a tree, all of whom were wrong. Philosophy provides the historical academic legitimacy for this approach of rationally working hard on one's most closely held concepts, delving into basic matters, and constructing theory based on that. We can see the role of philosophy informing physics, untangling the issues raised by quantum mechanics. So we suggest an analogy between economics, which uses physics' mathematics in much of its theoretical work, and physics. By discussing the very basis of what we are doing, keep our mind on where we are, as a zen master we have greater hope of overcoming the past analytical misfortunes of economics.

For example, economics debates often structure around key concepts. Perfect competition is overturned by Williamson's transactions cost approach. But perfect competition is kept as the surrounding analytical structure, and this is misleading. If the economists had taken the falasafa approach and started with the question, "what are the salient features of the system we are considering?", then we believe that this empirical observational approach would be bringing about a debate structure that has a better chance of reaching the Truth. This concept of structure of debate conditioning knowledge development is the argument of Thomas Kuhn's theory of knowledge in respect of "paradigm shifts". We can take this further and see that debate's course through time will be generated by structures of society, whether it is the rules of the language that ideas are communicated in or if political economy affects that actual choice of who is a valid person to produce knowledge and participate in the debate. So economics has taken a strongly mathematical turn since the 20th Century, perhaps because it produces arguments that reduce the number of people involved in the debate due to the ever increasing complexity of the mathematical language that is used to communicate in the debate. Those who argue in a different set of terms are disciplined or rejected with to the refrain 'this is not rigorous or analytical'. Thus the debate of economics is structured to maintain itself. There is no valid argument why the 'rigorous analysis' in other words putting economics into mathematics is necessarily going to lead one to the truth. The argument why logical reasoning from true assumptions will lead to true answers underlies the belief in mathematical economic theory, yet the mathematics is not suitable for society and distracts the basic problem of identifying the actual structures that exist and do effect outcomes in society.

From the rule 'economic theory must be rigorous (mathematical)' we see here an interesting fact, that conversations in the debates often repeat a similar set of refrains and junctures that lead to a certain structural stability to the social organisation of knowledge production and the path it takes. This is considered later when we look at long lasting social elements and propose the analytical tool of conversation trees, that is abstracting conversations between people that lead to a formation or reproduction of a social structure.

It would seem self-evident that science should be grounded in reality. This is the essence of every other science apart from economics. The biologist starts with the microscope, the astronomer starts with the telescope. While economists argue that their assumptions are grounded in slow changing "obvious" behavioural tendencies, such as profit maximisation/self interest, which we must add are highly likely to be specific to a historical period of capitalism, recent work on complex systems and even simple systems with feedback of certain orders and relations (nonlinear dynamics) shows that looking at a single aspect of the system without considering the complete reality is misleading. An iterative map can show structural change in its dynamics given certain small parameter changes. Why do we assume that the economy is not so contingently defined in its outcomes?

Thus we argue that in order to revitalise economics, we must consider as our starting point, a close analysis of the relevant aspects of the system. You may ask, where should we start? Clearly economics is different to other sciences because it is its relevance to society that determines what it should be about. Clearly economics has responded to social influences in terms of the problems it chooses to look at, a terribly problematic issue for all economists. When there was the Great Depression, there was the answer from Keynes, when there was inflation, there was Friedman. When there was a political desire for free trade, there was Adam Smith. But we want to take this a stage further. By answering the key questions, problems and issues society and the world faces, we can provide a guidance and a light for humanity. Building our observations on for example a question, such as "how does the housing market work?", which is highly relevant to today's world, we can see various institutions; estate agents, business media, home owners, home sellers, buy to let investors, property developers, tenants, home buyers. The dynamic produced by an institution is what could be termed the dialectic, in other words the process of relations between institutions, which is defined as the units of analysis in society. Economics is observationally about flows, whether monetary, informational or in terms of assets, activity and beliefs. A key point to add to any analysis is where these flows feedback among institutions, gives rise to developments of various things such as consensus, value, sudden change like crashes or booms.

The role of falasafa in economics is ongoing, it is not just about setting the structure for the debate. Many debates depend on our terms and the contradictions in opinion are explained by this. The idea of "productive and unproductive" activity in an economy affects the rent seeking debate among others. Thus such a debate would benefit from falasafa's wise intervention in defining productive activity. This question can be seen to depend on what we mean by the economy or specifically capitalism. Essentially we take the point that capitalism is about generating high, long term, growing levels of activity in society and among them, through monetary compensation and the corresponding affect this has on social status and reproduction of institutions like classes. We have a hypothesis for theory and empiricism to consider, which is that capitalism provides better results than state planning in many sectors of the economy because of the presence of feedback between flows and institutions that lead to growing yet often volatile results in statistics such as GDP, asset prices/quantity and thus wealth, employment, wages, profits to firms.

It would be useful to apply falasafa to the understanding of inflation. Consider for example whether the rise in price of a product due to better marketing of it, quality changes or just the passage of time providing greater popularity of it, is inflation or a rise in GDP?

Consider what falasafa can do for the question of growth in the money supply. Evidence shows that large increases in the money supply lead to hyperinflation in many cases. Falasafa thinking leads one to believe that the system of money flowing around the economy becomes unstable and ever increasing if money supply is allowed to grow considerably. Keeping a reasonably tight grip on the money supply thus leads to system stability, which may or may not be desirable. We consider later whether the historically generated concept of time value of money (discounting of cash flows with time) and debt with interest leads to this instability.

We have thus shown a few areas where more in depth thinking based on observational reality may lead one to consider a whole new debating and methodological process as well as give rise to a fertile market of theories competing for evidence. We can only hope that this is the way forward for economics.

3. Counterfactuals in Life History Livelihood Studies of Poverty

Abstract

A modern trend in the literature on poverty has been to extract life histories of the poor. These detailed narratives obtained through interviews have a weakness. They do not elucidate the counterfactuals in the life history, that is what would have happened if some factors were different and therefore do not give a good indication of the appropriate policy to be undertaken to provide escape routes from poverty. We outline an approach that can be used to show the alternatives through financial modelling in spreadsheets of alternative scenarios. Therefore advice and intervention can be structured by poverty eliminating organisations.

Argument

Life histories, or a narrative of the history of a poor person are frequently created by academics interested in understanding poverty. These are normally part of a larger livelihood analysis often combined with panel and cross sectional data to bring out qualitative facts. They also have the advantage of communicating the difficulties of the poor as well as giving tried and tested escape routes from deprivation.

They do not however give an indication of what would have happened if different courses and decisions were taken. In short, what are the choices of the poor and what are the necessary tendencies of different categories of poor's life histories. This is known as the counterfactual. The term comes from the philosophy of physics and is used to understand the contradictions and problems of quantum mechanics. It's application comes from the study of history. In order to suggest that say a country has had growing inequality due to liberalisation it is necessary to know what would have happened otherwise. It is certain that this is not something that can be found objectively, that can be measured with accuracy, however, an indication of the likely outcome could be found using a method used by financial analysts. In the financial world, practitioners often need to find out whether a project would be viable under different scenarios. In order to make an assessment of this they use spreadsheet models of the financial aspects of a project and run this under different assumptions.

We argue that this could be a useful way to expose the counterfactuals in the life histories of the poor. Simply, a model of the assets, income streams and outgoings are taken with the life history interview. An indication of possible income streams and asset accumulation is found by sampling regions with those opportunities that are accessible to the poor person who is being studied. It might be possible to find out that certain forms of education produced positive alternative life histories, though this would alter the outgoings and short term income of the subject. New ideas to find escape routes from poverty could come about.

Alternative viewpoints

The limitation and thus the thrust of future innovation in poverty research is to assess the macro impact of alternative life history strategies. That is for example, if everyone was to become a doctor then there would be oversupply and thus many unemployed, whereas the individual decision to become a doctor would improve the life history of the individual as well as her/his community. The need to niche (each person doing different things to make money) is therefore apparent from this statement, thus policy drawn from counterfactual life history analysis requires a heterogeneous policy outcome. This means that policy must find many different sources of incomes and assets for the poor with care taken that the collective result is not self-destroying.

4. Kaldor's Laws vs Keynes

What would a synthesis of Keynes and Kaldor look like? The processes of supply are that different firms impact each other, though manufacturing does this better since a product can be mass produced. Thus a factory can produce over time many copies of a product which can have high value added. Therefore a manufacturing firm will have increasing returns to scale given a high demand for its product. Supply is assumed to not necessarily create its own demand. The fact that a company has fixed costs is the reason why there is increasing returns to scale, since at low levels of sales the company breaks even. At high levels of sale, where the product becomes a cultural contagion, profits are much higher. We posit that this is a more important channel of growth than the physical change in the amount of materials that can be made. This is clearly important but we believe that the financial supersedes the physical.

When we look at Keynes, i.e. demand feedback throughout the economy, we want to disaggregate this and look at individual firms and individuals each connected to each other with goods and money flowing between each other. Let us assume there has been a rise in the stock market, so there is more money potentially to flow around the system. The demand for a well marketed good rises and so industry grows. At some point it increases its scale, therefore there is more to invest in the firm. The key point is that it is because the firm is a value generating process, it adds substantial value to inputs, that means there is increasing returns.

The non-manufacturing sector will have an increase in its income from the expenditure of the workforce and owners of the manufacturing firm. Thus there is a rise in overall GDP. Since the manufacturer has increased profits there will be substantially more demand by those connected into the output of money from the firm for goods which are culturally contagious (e.g. phones, TV, computers, cars, homes, stocks) as well as services. Will this lead to greater productivity in the non-manufacturing sector? Clearly one must distinguish between products which are services (like hair cuts) and products which are not manufactured but are assets, such as houses and stocks. Also one must distinguish between physical productivity and profit per worker (price productivity).

If a firm makes more phones for every worker it has then there is a clear example of more physical productivity. However making phones is not what a firm does, making money is its essential role. If a firm makes a change to a phone that enhances its value to the customer, such as 3G, then it is increasing the profit per worker as well. One could say that this is about changes in quality, but we would say that quality is how well something works rather than what it does for the consumer, whether this is in terms of status (like a Rolls Royce) or in terms of changing their life (e.g. a mobile phone rather than a landline). When we measure productivity in growth accounting we often use GDP data which is partly caused by physical productivity and mostly caused by the amount of value has been added by the firm. Thus there is a lapse of logic in how economists talk about the supply side with monetary terms. Accounting for inflation has no effect on this, as if taking the price of a basket of goods that might be purchased by a consumer would make any sense, apart from eliminate some of the price feedback (the rise in prices due to the rise in prices) that occurs in this data. Inflation adjustment entails throwing the baby out with the bathwater since some price increases, such as for better innovations or marketing, are important to capitalist economic growth.

Returning to our original discussion about whether services would increase in productivity, it is unlikely that they would improve their physical productivity except in the small way of improving skills in a workforce through greater practice. On the other hand, price productivity is likely to improve since profits are rising when there is greater demand and this may rise by an increasing amount per worker depending on how the capital labour mix for the provision of a service.

When firms are doing well in the economy the value of buying a stake in those firms increases. As a firm is sold, another may be bought by the owners thus bringing up the value of all firms if this occurs in a large way. In addition, other assets may be invested in by the people who are connected to the output stream of profit from the firm.

Given the strategy of banks to lend more to those with greater assets it would seem that a rise in demand filters through to more lending since asset prices would have increased. This raises demand in the economy.

Thus we see the progress of a pound throughout the economy that generates the expansive growth of capitalism.

5. Memetic house prices

Memetics is the study of units of information (meme) flowing around a society that reaches what has been understood in the economics literature as contagion, that is the widespread adoption of a belief or practice. An example of a meme is religion, which spreads widely as an accepted form of truth. Other examples are scientism and liberalism which are a widely accepted contagion in the Western world. Society is seen as a network of agents each spreading memes that they have internalised to others. A problematic point of this analysis is what happens when two equally credible memes that are mutually exclusive exist. Which one would dominate?

All that is necessary for a contagion to occur is the ability of an idea (meme) to spread between agents in a society. Structural aspects of a market, such as lack of supply of houses and the desire to compete for higher prices when supply is short, will be a driver for this spread of the idea of 'rising house prices'. However, the covetous nature of modern society is also a part of the rise in house prices meme spreading, since people who did not desire more wealth would not look for higher house prices when they sell. The greed of society, modelled in consumer choice as monotonicity of the utility function, is itself a meme which has spread since the medieval times of Europe when such things were seen as sinful for the average person.

If such an analysis is correct then one might argue that it would be in the interests of house buyers to spread a meme that there are falling house prices. However, buyers are future sellers, that is they are co-opted into the house price rise meme by the belief that house prices will rise further in the future when they can sell. Thus there is a lack of competition among memes and therefore the housing market rises over time, even ahead of reasonable indicators such as house price to earnings ratios.

6. Economic theorisation

Bourdeiu's cried out against the mathematical sickness of economics in its modern form. He talked of models that were description rather than deduction. In this he means we should take a more empirical look, though he is interpreted by us to mean casual as well as rigorous empiricism. By casual empiricism we mean the capability of the human mind to observe and note key facts that determine an object of interest. We will argue that deductive reasoning is no different to this approach, we posit that economists are preoccupied with obtaining ideological results and fit their 'reasoning' to the answer they wish to find. We consider the debacle created by Dinwiddy in showing that the State is as efficient as the Market using general equilibrium analysis. The key to understanding why Dinwiddy was able to turn the main thrust of economic theory on its head, a work of deep insight and imagination, is to understand that she put the state into the general equilibrium equations where the firm would normally be and replaced prices in this equation with a factor that could be determined when making a decision about how much resources the state should spend. This roundly put the whole of general equilibrium theory to its grave, since it becomes clear that the reasoning produces a result similar to the ontological argument for God. This is based on the assumption of man is imperfect and God is perfect. Since man exists, cogito ergo sum, God exists, since perfection has all of the positive qualities of imperfection. The flaw in this argument is that one could have a perfect imaginary island, which would then exist by virtue of the assumption of perfection even though it is imaginary. So to get back to general equilibrium theory, the firm is God in the ontological argument. It produces perfect results due to the nature of the logical machine that produces a deduction that is true but does not really tell us why firms are capable institutions for the production of goods. In essence in setting up the system of reasoning in a model one is applying one's casual observations of the economy. For example, the idea that agents are profit maximising and the attached idea that this can be modelled as a mathematical maximisation problem.

The second issue is that a common desire of economics, even historical types, is to use rigorous empiricism to isolate causes of change. This should be the end result of economics but it is not the first stage of analysis, which is identification of the system in question. An example of rigorous empiricism is to essentially partition countries into those with high and low growth and then attach causality to any variable that is of high value in the high growth country set. For example, human capital is high in rich countries. It therefore becomes a result of regression analysis that human capital is seen to cause growth. On the other hand lack of corruption is high in high growth countries so this is seen as the cause of growth. Barro's regression of inflation/growth to independence of the monetary authorities is another one. However, such analysis becomes tediously nonsensical when the many causes of growth are put together. If single exogenous variable regression gives us the confirmation of causality then why can one find many causes; lack of corruption, human capital, monetary institutional independence. The retort to this argument is that one can have a multivariate regression containing all variables. However one should realise that statistics was developed prior to what we know about non-linear dynamics, which tells us that what appears random can be deterministic. All statistics depends on a meta-model of randomness, i.e. variables distributed by some or other distribution. Were the economic system to have any chaotic equations within it then statistics would not be suitable for determining cause since some of the randomness which is stripped out by the regression would in fact be a part of the causal system. Clearly exogenous variables must be independent under the assumptions of regression so it is possible that variables may interact which means that the whole process of rigorous empiricism through regression is in need of redevelopment.

Proving the likelihood of chaos in economic systems requires some element of this system to be subject to non-linear interactions between variables or feedback which is non-linear. An example is interest and profit paths. Vernon's product life cycle hypothesis suggests that profit will go up a significant rate at first. This can be assumed to be greater than the cost of capital, the loan going up by a constant interest rate. As long as this happens (and it is likely to be so since the firm would not engage in developing the product otherwise) the profit after interest payments goes up possibly by a non-linear amount. This money is recycled into the economy as savings and costs such as wages. In effect wealth is created by producing products but all costs are repaid and added to the economy. The level of economic growth increases. However, there is feedback between the amount of investment (savings) and profits produced. The more money available for investment from banks, the more profits there are. And since profit goes up by a much higher amount than the interest rate cost, there is a possible non-linear causal connection. The successful company may also be bought up by investors, which raises the level of wealth in the economy since an asset (the company) has been created. Thus wealth increases, profits increase, and bank earnings from interest also rise when a new product is produced.

The fundamental equations of financial value generation by the firm (Finance/Supply)
National Income = profit + cost of capital + wages + land costs

Profit = f(capital)

Capital = g(wealth)   ; the more wealth one has the more capital one can raise

Wealth = h (profit)   ; the assets of a company are worth more if they are making higher profit

Fundamental Psychological/cultural value generation by the firm (Demand)

Cultural want - Meme – Product benefits - Product – Firm Image   ; meme complex (M) of want and firm

M circulates through networks powered by social and symbolic capital of all nodes in the network who are co-opted into the firm. For example, a journalist may write an article about the product. Over time, M becomes a consensus and is a cultural unit in itself that is self-evidently propagated. An example is make up or the hoover (which has as the name of the product the company that invented it).

7. Inflation and assets

Inflation is not a reality. It is an imposed idealisation put upon data to reduce the primacy of money. Money is what is moving throughout an economy in a feedback process, moving from person to person, stimulating them into activity that is useful for others. Inflation, given by an average basket of goods does show a phenomena of price feedback, that is prices that depend on other prices, but it is an overstated problem. For example, in harsh times people will switch consumption to cheaper goods, goods which may be of a lower quality. Thus the uncertainty of knowing the right basket of goods to calculate inflation is apparent.

Thus we can see that the difference between real and non-real growth is near impossible to calculate. Thus we see the primacy of money in an economy. When we unlock ourselves from the inflationary chains we see that things like assets become deeply important for the economy. Looking at inflation adjusted income we would see asset rises as a decline in the growth of the economy. But rather they are the source of development. The myriad channels in which assets raise the amount of money in the economy combined with the fact that asset prices, while increased by the amount of money that goes into the asset market, can go much higher than the total amount of money in the economy. This is because only a small proportion of assets are traded at any one time. Thus most of the assets are held in expectation of capital growth or because they have a useful cultural value, like houses.

It is understood that inflation is linked to the time value of money. The latter is the value by which money is risklessly assumed to increase over time. This must be seen as culturally and historically contingent. In an Islamic economy, the presence of a decrease in savings over time due to the law of Zakat, that 2.5% of all savings not invested is given to the poor or needy, changes this concept.

Inflationary pressure can be caused by rises in the interest rate. As much as firms leverage their investments, there will be a cost push effect of rises in interest rates by the same argument that wage rises lead to inflation. If prices rise by the same proportion that interest rates rise then there is a lowering of the real interest rate, given that firms are able to restrict competitive pressures that would avoid price rises through norms and system wide strategic compliance. This line of thinking leads us to question the very basis of the theory underlying monetary policy in conjunction with labour market theory. The conventional wisdom is that rises in interest rates lead to a fall in inflation. Yet they can also be considered, assuming one wishes coherence with Labour market theory, to do the opposite. It is an interesting hypothesis to consider whether in fact the transmission of monetary policy is through changing the amount of money circulating through the system, which in fact is how central banks change interest rates.

If we take it as given that it is money circulation that is proportionate to the amount of economic activity, then we can look at the scenario where Zakat is introduced in an economy that does not allow interest to be paid on loans. The investor has a choice of either losing 2.5% per year of their money or risking their capital through engaging or investing in business. The third alternative is to give interest free loans, which though they would not involve reduction in the value of their capital, would not allow any increase in it either. Large, established organisations such as government would be seen by the investor to be low risk investments and therefore they may find it acceptable to lend interest free loans to them. Thus fiscal policy in an interest free economy needs zakat as a law to be viable. Since the investor wishes to develop their capital, they would also invest in value adding processes such as businesses, perhaps by way of intermediary organisations which would essentially be a cross between venture capital funds and a bank. On the other hand, unproductive assets, such as houses, would not be of great interest to the investor except as much as they are needed for social institutional reproduction. We would expect that money would not be heavily drawn to such assets and for their price to be largely stable over long periods of time, except as population and income changes occurred. Thus we would expect house prices in this kind of economy to remain within the income of the buyers. Government could use fiscal policy to give loans to people to buy houses, which would be interest free as well.

Consider now the effect of an increase in the money supply. The key determinant of the outcome is the recipient of the increase in money. But the recipient is a tree of people and organisations that each pass on the increase in money supply to others, since saving is discouraged, while investment in value adding profitable avenues is enforced into the system. It would seem a possibility that inflation may not be a necessary consequence for anything less than very large rises in the money supply as a proportion of the economy. Were this shown to be true, the consequences for humanity would be nothing short of astounding. Consider the fact that when the money supply in Spain rose following conquest of parts of the Americas there was according to Montesquieu inflation, but when money supply rose in the early Islamic empire following conquests of parts of Africa and Europe there was economic growth according to the literature. In both cases money supply was determined by the amount of gold/silver in circulation and thus conquest brought new sources of these precious metals. This insight proceeds from our earlier contention that a matrix of nodes connecting to each other unidirectionally can be summarised as a triangle of nodes that will either have an ever increasing, stable or decreasing rate of change in the flow of money between them. Under the system of zakat there is a deflating aspect to the system which has the result of raising the market size since zakat is given to the poor. Thus the system does not see the booms and bubbles of contemporary capitalism but instead we can feel that money supply increases from government can lead to stable sustained growth.

8. Debt and Balance of Payments

Many developing countries have high levels of debt. There seems to be large amounts of particularly foreign denominated debt held by governments in these nations. We suggest that the reason for this may be a feedback compounding process that raises the level of foreign denominated debt held over time very quickly.

The process is as follows; foreign debt is taken which goes up by its interest rate. As the debt interest is paid, the exchange rate devalues, due to the massive exchange of money required to pay the debt interest off. This puts the balance of payments into deficit, which itself must be financed by debt, which in turn increases the interest payments. Overall the debt increases taking an ever larger part of the state's expenditure and leads to default eventually. Therefore the international financial structure leads to a tendency to debt crises.

9. On the dynamic system of the economy

The economy can be seen as a matrix of agents where each element of the matrix represents the bank account of each agent (Agent matrix). Another matrix determines the percentage of money that flows (spending) to each agent from each agent (transformation matrix, $T(t(i), t(j))$ where $1 > t(i), t(j) > 0$). The agent matrix is multiplied by the transformation matrix repeatedly each period. What is noticeable is that while the bank accounts of each matrix goes up, the overall level of money in the economy has not changed. This is what we could call wealth growth. However, economic (income) growth can be either from rises in the value of the bank account assets (like house price rises) or from more transactions occurring or from debt being introduced into the system which changes the transformation matrix so that the sum of each agent's spending is greater than 1.

Sinks can be represented in this formulation as agents which have many if not all other agents spending much of their money on them. Houses are a sink in fact all assets are, but when they draw money towards them they become larger in value thus creating conditions whereby there is an outflow of money from houses into the economy.

10. On the nature of the economy

When a firm produces a product that has a large customer base and makes a profit, the value of the firm itself as an asset becomes large. This adds to the wealth of the economy, when the sale of the firm is realised. Also a bank will lend money on the basis of the value of the business thus unlocking the savings of the economy. Developing countries have fewer businesses making less money thus savings are not loaned to their fullest amount. The money multiplier, where bank loans become spending and thus deposits in accounts and therefore are recycled into the economy over and over again, does not come into effect in its fullest form therefore the developing country is stuck in a low income and low wealth steady state.

When a firm engages in marketing it creates new blocks of value in the culture of society and in terms of the economic framework, creates a monetary linkage to their product. People come to yearn and save up for those products, which become a part of existence. But there is a limited amount of goods that can be known about and bought by a consumer. Each person has a finite amount of brain capacity and also time to buy products, so there is a limited amount of goods that can exist in the brain and also one cannot shop for 1 billion products. Therefore the economy has a ceiling level of value which it cannot go above given a certain number of consumers. However, by increasing the amount of consumers this ceiling can be raised. A way of doing this is to develop poorer places and end poverty.

11. The world bank and poverty lines

The world bank estimates that there are 1 billion people who are poor, who live on less than a $1 per day. This implies that giving $1 to each of these people will get them out of poverty. The end of poverty is easily achievable for only $1 billion per day or $365 billion per year. This lowering of the poverty line, the level at which one is considered to be poor, is part of the mean and stingy policy of the right wing that has always been the case in history. Why should not the poor have washing machines, nice clothes, a mobile phone, computers, money for their pension, healthcare, education up to degree level? Why can't poverty be defined as not having many of the items that society can produce that would improve welfare up to a reasonable standard. Why can't this be the goal?

12. Systems of thought

In parallel to the system of signs of Saussure, the differences between the interplay of the many signifieds and signifiers, we suggest the idea map. These are networks of ideas, linked together by mental observation, subjectively. The idea map is related to the arguments it generates. These arguments are associated with interests through the idea map, so an economic theory that says that minimum wages leads to unemployment is to link the interest of the worker in not being unemployed with the idea that one should not have minimum wages. In society, an advance has been made so that idea maps are also the product of social forces trying to achieve consensus. The right wing elements of society may generate the idea map that minimum wages lead to unemployment so that the left will not push for the minimum wage as it will cause a bad effect for workers, the left's interest. Idea maps' links are not necessarily causality but can be any subjective link that makes ideas connected, as in the case of interdisciplinary social science. They is an interplay between the idea map and the arguments it creates. These arguments form the interests of the believer in the idea map.

The idea map has tensions inside it which when conceived as an idea map, such as interdisciplinary social science (composed of sociology, political economy, semiotics, post-structuralism, etc) can lead to people changing the ideas to alleviate these tensions.

The idea map is drawn and redrawn by each individual participant and is propagated. Idea maps does not necessarily entail knowledge, they are identifiable in political movements and coalitions, in advertising as an entirety and in the network of associations in ordinary advertising. They are the building blocks of ideology. They are our values and they are a valuable tool to help one look clearly at much of the linguistic reality of society.

An advert for a soft drink may be linked to ideas in culture of youth in general, of the higher social strata of youth culture (coolness) and of the feelings one obtains from consuming this product. This becomes associated with the brand and propagates as an idea map through the coincidence of minds filled with that idea map which is the result of advertising in the media affecting many people. Idea maps generate value, that is the creation of demand both potential and realisable. The supply of money to allow value to be realised, that is become part of the circulation of money, is not generated by idea maps in the realm of advertising. Some idea maps do not need to be advertised to be generated. Google is a useful technological information product which is free and thus creates value in the sense that it generates an audience from the idea map it's brand is constituted of. The Google idea map is "find any information you require from a large mass of information" and "simple easy to use interface" and "minimalism", an artistic movement in culture and "quick loading web page". This is propagated across the internet and among people and has generated a market leader in the search engine market without conventional advertising. These associations are instantly and cross culturally made by most if not all observers. They have the characteristic of an objective idea map while the earlier soft drink ad idea map has the characteristic of a subjective media created one.

Arguments are created by the Google idea map such as "it is better than its competitors" while the soft drinks ad creates the same argument. "You should use this product" is the general argument produced by a successful brand's idea map. This argument is propagated around society through the spread of idea map. At the grand level, they produce legitimacy. "You should buy capitalism".

There is a dyad of idea map and argument which creates Gramscian interests. The fact that there are contrasting interests in society changes the idea maps to alter the arguments which themselves determine interests.

The memetic analysis of idea map propagation would suggest that idea maps which are most likely to propagate will become the most widely spread. If an idea map is in line with an interest in a social force then the members of that group will find themselves taking up the idea map. The survival value of an idea map is ultimately the relationship the arguments from the idea map have with the interests of different groups in society. If these arguments depend on hypothetical information then if this information is later found there will be a discarding of the idea map. Fads and fashions occur in idea maps, witness the change from Marxism to Post-modernism in elements of the left. This is part of the flux and flow, non-linear dynamic system of ideas in the society. Feedback at tipping points will lead to different ideas coming into favour and losing them as people are more likely to hold an idea if someone else is propagating them that they are linked to and they find to be credible. Idea maps can be long and complex, this may add to the fascination for a potential believer. In fact the most privileged of idea maps, science, is totally inaccessible to all but the few. Thus we are in contravention of the memetic theory of Dawkins. In a sense we can reconcile ourselves with Dawkins by suggesting that the word "Science" with its de facto idea map, of truth, progress and modernity, propagates around the system as a short message which is credible due to the inventions it has created which generates credibility for the idea maps of science which do not propagate throughout the whole of society. Thus people pay money to learn to become scientists. Idea maps are associations in the mind that spread through society. They are the very meaning of things which is where they are related to signs in that idea maps have meanings drawn from them. Thus we are at odds with Semiotics which we believe has missed this important way of looking at society. Semiotics deals with the sign as it is already conceived but says nothing about the actual development of meaning. Even the study of how children learn signs is not the approach to the totality of knowledge. Meaning is culturally and historically determined in the development of idea maps. The presence of rationality makes idea maps alter over time as they are debated and formed and reformed, with irrational ideas being discarded. The cultural narrative of progress leads to idea maps being changed to the march of time, with new ideas being created and links between ideas being altered. Idea maps overlap, forming meta-narratives, like anti-Americanism or modernity. They can become dissociated with the ideas they originally came from and change under another dynamic, one of the social groups which are involved in the debate of the idea map and thus create a hyperreality. They lose their credibility and grounding as their origin is lost, as can be seen in the stories of the news media which are many different idea maps that are propelled by interests of participants in society, and echo in each other in debate among members of the media.

Debate is a form where idea maps can be drawn and redrawn but also where different idea maps can come into contact through the medium of argument. These arguments interact to form the debate. The progress of this is to a more complex form of thought than the idea map. Ideas are created in debate, the product of many limited minds working together to form a greater whole. These go on to form the basis for new idea maps and if the debate is propagated well, to change the idea maps of society.

The game of the debate where each side wishes to win, which means to show the superiority of their idea maps leads to fixing of facts to ideas, and moulding of idea maps into arguments which support their side of the debate. Interests will converge in debate as the interaction between the participants leads to each side wanting to convince the other in order to win. Thus debate leads to consensus being produced. Arguments that are difficult to overcome in debate will lead to people trying to change idea maps by blocking or disregarding some lines of thought to undermine whole sections of idea maps in addition to countering individual arguments. The example is Popper's use of the Hegelian Dialectic to create his argument that democracy was the best system, which uses the same reasoning base as Marx to come to a mutually exclusive outcome. Thus we see that ideas have a reasoning base, which forms part of the production of the idea map. This may or may not be associated with the interest of the group. Many reasoning bases will come from a stock of tools which are recognised by the group which seeks to make the argument. In this, Popper is rare. Economists use the tools of science to create idea maps which create arguments that capitalism is good. These tools of science are part of modernity which is part of capitalism and democracy. This is the idea map for western society (modernity- capitalism- democracy). There is an interest in western society to propagate democracy across the world. It has not been seen that the best way to do this is to make democracy better, so that it solves the world's problems. This would come from looking at the idea of modernity that is progress which involves continual creative destruction. Democracy does not mutate with new generations. It is reproduced in its archetypal form through each generation. Strange that democracy is centrally about discussion of new ideas yet it does not discuss itself to any large degree.

Where is truth in all this discussion? We have belief of participants in debate but does this tend towards the truth. We should look at how debate tends away from the truth. This can happen through the production of idea maps that conform to an interest or are part of the game of debate. We can also approach this problem from the standpoint of analysis of the outcome of a reasoning base. This is a methodology, a set of practices and rules which govern the creation of ideas. Reasoning bases which engage in criticism will from Popper come nearer to the truth. Distributed computing would tell us that complex problems can be solved by many agents each attacking a small section of the problem. Debate allocates the problem to many participants. A person comes up with an argument which is countered by someone else. This creates an opportunity for another to see the problem in a different way and synthesise the two arguments. Another sees the synthesis as valid but part of it is wrong. So they suggest a new revision to the idea. An amendment. Another sees another problem with this. Someone else suggests a paradigm shift. The idea maps are changed and the process continues. We can see from this example that debate can be modelled as a distributed computing process even though the problem is not subdivided by a central controller. The mechanism in debate is completely decentralised and created by debate.

Back to our question of where is truth, it can be seen that ideas such as mathematics are generated by the practice of mathematics and the very essence of the logical rules that they form. Thus there is a system external to society in the essence of thought which is the generator of the idea of mathematics. Different people can thus find similar ideas without communication, simply by following the rules of logic. The interaction between the person and the mathematical system allows that person to have the idea of mathematics. This is distinct from ideas such as a mathematical hypothesis such as the Riemann hypothesis or the idea of God, which do not stem necessarily from the external system (in the case of mathematics, the rules of logic and the system of rules and methodology of it) but are created within society and propagate for reasons other than an external system.

The truth in this analysis has the characteristic of coming from an external system that generates ideas. Given that mathematics is truth. Inductive logic from scientific experiments can be seen to be a kind of external system as well. What other kinds of external systems are there? And what of the problem of the external system of society that generates truths about society? This is deeply problematic since there can be no external system that does this since the only system that can do this is society itself. However, since one is part of society no complete revelation of the system of society can occur since we are the model and must interact with it. One needs God to find truth in society. That said one can observe parts of society, or even the society as a whole (which is different from the society of individuals) and use that to generate ideas. The question is, what is the appropriate methodology for social science and policy analysis, given that there are many different methodologies in social science and these have changed over time?

One idea is to abstract mechanisms and structures in society from data, whether from narrative, or numbers or qualities or simply from casual observation. Define relationships, though not necessarily causality or the exact degree of control a node has on another node. Try this for other examples, different places, different times, different circumstances in others words carry out "experiments". See if you can find the general structure and also the specific relationships. At the most specific you will create the historical narrative, the relationship will be valid for a experiment set of 1. At the most general, few relationships will be valid for all 'experiments', but the experiment set will possibly be sub dividable into different groups. You will need to play around with the categories and concepts you use to develop the relationships. Change the very basis of your thinking and carry out the experiments again. Try to synthesise your findings and come up with a general structure that governs most if not all of your experiments. Subject your ideas to criticism and debate. Take ideas from the debate and discard ideas that do not stand the pressure of criticism. This kind of methodology will create ideas from the external system of society through essentially following a distributed problem solving approach. Society is partitioned into different experiments which are 'solved' for relationships and then the whole result is connected together by the researcher.

13. The production function

The capitalist production function is seen to be a predictor of growth built on analytical foundations of neo-classical economics. We must diverge from discussing this to a thought concerning the unwritten methodology of successful progressive sciences, rather than the Stalinist Bureaucracy that we term the economics profession. Every single science that has made any progress in the last century has one simple, basic commandment. Look. Look at the object of enquiry. Do not pluck ideas from the air. Essentially this is the objective-subjective distinction, with successful science erring on the path of objectivity. Yet economists have consistently and insanely taken the opposite view, with a litany of excuses as to why this is so. Biologists begin their study with a microscope, Astronomers begin with a telescope. Close observation is the essence of successful science.

Observation of society would produce some facts. The first of these is that society is full of human beings. These people are connected through institutions. Flows of various valued objects occur between them governed by those institutions; goods, money, assets, love, true and untrue information, ideas for reform of institutions, etc. These flows, in abstraction, can satisfactorily be referred to as a network. So we have an analytical representation that no amount of calculus would ever produce. There is the true story of the statistician who asked his advanced students to produce the law for data that he had generated from Pythagoras' theorem using only statistical techniques. They could not find even this simple law from the data set without having been told how it was generated.

National income is a piece of data in the units of a currency. It is often calculated as the value added by the economy and is thus a misleading statistic on economic activity and flows since this is essentially data collected from VAT returns supplied by businesses in the UK. The problem lies in the fact that labour costs are part of the added value figure, they do not form part of the calculation of costs in the UK. Thus increasing labour in the amount of value added and thus GDP leads to circularity in the production function, since $Y=f(K,L)$. This is therefore not an equation that can be statistically estimated within the assumptions of such an analysis, since the causal route of labour to income is necessarily in the inflation of value added estimates in addition to higher levels of production and demand. Consider for example, falling wages because of weak labour power, this would lead to, holding the system frozen, the same level of physical output (volume) with falling national income since value added in terms of labour's wages are lower. But the capitalist profit = wages – cost. Thus if costs remain the same and wages fall, profit will increase. Therefore national income in monetary terms will not be changed in Truth, but will be lower as it is measured. If we suggest a simple political economic model of labour power having a monotonic relationship with wages then clearly whenever labour power gets stronger, value added will rise more if labour power becomes stronger and the market is amenable to price or quantity rises in production. The choice of price rises rather than quantity rises to provide largesse to labour leads to inflation and growth (and thus higher interest rates from independent central banks) in the former case and growth in terms of GDP volume in the latter. If one's economy is full of classically rational firms then they will have to judge between raising prices, which does not raise profits since interest rates will rise in response to this, or raising quantity, which means raising productivity or raising the amount of labour employed whilst stimulating demand.

This is possibly why central banks do not do GDP targeting but rather inflation targeting.

The second point of the aggregate production function is that it does not occur in the planning of any business in any part of the world. It is not derived from any observation of any business. Since the market has a tendency towards adopting better techniques it is unclear why they would not use publicly available aggregate production functions whether in financial planning and budgeting or in decision making of choosing between various techniques, were the production function a truthful device. Since the market does not use this, what is the justification for the market acting as if it did use this technique? Appeals to non-existent theoretical structures cannot repeal the objective truth of the higher court of empiricism.

The third point is in the empirical application of production functions in "Growth Accounting". The problem with this is the main result of this research, namely that most of the increase in growth is not accounted for by labour or capital but is rather held in a residual to the equation. This residual is precisely the problem, capital and labour are not the only determinant of growth, thus the production function does not actually explain anything or tell us anything. More recent research has brought up many examples of different explanations for growth, such as human capital formation, stable open markets, respect of property rights and the insulation of the state. The circularity of the equations matches the many laps of the circuits of capital in the world with endogenous growth theory (growth comes from growth).

We have outlined our key observation concerning the failing methodology of economists, namely lack of observation. But in addition to this we may add some less obvious criticisms. Firstly, there is the tendency to desire to be too exact in relations of entities of analysis. Secondly, there is the overestimation of overlapping models to each be objective truth since they are derived from seemingly obvious assumptions. I see two objects and say since 1+1 =2 then these two objects must be two different entities. But in fact my problem was in my very understanding of the existence of the objects, since what I was looking at was Yin and Yang, which as every wise person knows are one and the same object. Overlapping models should in debate be connected in terms of nesting within one another, one being discarded in favour of another or being left as a confusing conundrum for later scholars to deal with. The fact is that in economics multiple models exist in a variety of different analytical fields to explain the same phenomena, with no one model really trying to become dominant in any particular area. Game theory sits alongside neo-classical economics. In order to rationalise this with the fact that economists trust their logic and assumptions, it is held in reason that if assumption and logic are correct then the outcome must be correct, then we may rescue economics from it's daze by nesting our methodology with the rest of economics. This is that the logic-assumptions axis is really talking about processes within society that may or may not be empirically observable in dominance or even at all. Thus we do not say that there is not a price mechanism. Instead we say that it is possible to see the effects of higher prices from demand outstripping supply. At times this simple device may be in effect. At times it may not. The key point is that there are assumed to be many processes working through society which do have a logical path, they form and are destroyed, may be long lived or short lived. Just as Yin and Yang, good turning into bad and then back again forever, are also a possible process in society. The fact that economics can produce parallel models for the same objects of enquiry without any clear indication of one model being wrong and the other being right, given that all economic models are true in assumption and logic, means that, since the world is assumed to be a manifestation of logic, many processes can occur in society in parallel, in a network, all in flux.

14. On the normal distribution

The normal distribution is a term in statistics that gives the properties of independent random variables, for example, what proportion of values these groups of these variables will take, or the estimation of the average (mean) from a sample. It is a cornerstone of statistics and therefore science which needs the normal distribution to test theories empirically. It is based on a rigorous proof, the central limit theorem.

We argue that this foundation stone of science and mathematics is wrong. We suggest that the very conceptualisation of randomness is a result of our flawed knowledge which leads us to this mathematical artefact (something which exists in mathematic logic but not in reality).

Firstly, the assumption is that there are independent randomly distributed variables is in dispute. A system may produce what appears to be random results when in fact they are the result of a chaotic non-linear system. Thus what appears to be random is in fact determined. A system may be highly influenced by a chaotic non-linear system which leads to variables which are partly determined and thus have a definite non-random element. These kinds of systems can occur wherever there is feedback of variables (due to the chaotic properties of some iterative maps) thus the distribution of the variables is in fact not independent of the values they take. In economics many variables are in fact 'counters', they are the store of other variables, like a bank balance going up with income over time. A distribution of a person's wealth will go up over time, thus shifting towards the positive side. The mean goes up over a lifetime.

The class structure of society will determine the cross-sectional distribution of income, one would expect business people to earn more than the unemployed. Therefore a cross-sectional distribution of income would not conform to the assumptions of the normal distribution since the variable, income, is not a random variable. Money does not randomly flow to people but is rather the product of capital distribution. A rise in incomes due to the poor having capital allocated to them will produce a change in income that is not the result of a random process. In essence, the abuse of the normal distribution veers us away from enhancing scientific knowledge.

We now question the very idea of randomness. It seems an unscientific concept, since what is called randomness is the sum total of things we do not know and cannot conceive at present. The idea that random consequences cancel each other out on average denies the likelihood of the unlikely. The fact of the matter is that one cannot actually determine things which are indeterminate. Some phenomena can only be modelled in terms of simple networks of mutually caused variables which do not have any determined outcome.

The weakness in this argument is that the normal distribution is the best tool we have. But it does not get us closer to the truth rather it imposes a subjective reality onto the system. There is a question as to whether information about the system is contained in variables which are observed. An example is the story of the maths students who were shown a data set generated from Pythagoras' theorem but instead made a model using statistical tools that only predicted the existing data set rather than finding Pythagoras' theorem. The question of how much information is contained in variables cannot be understood by mathematics alone. Rather a science of testing the validity of statistics must begin, which looks at different classes of well understood systems and sees how well statistics can determine the real system dynamics. In this way improvements could be made to statistics and its methodology that would have wide reaching consequences for knowledge in general.

15. The theory of the Islamic state

"the meaning of life is the meaning of the state"

Abstract

"the theory of the Islamic state is deduced from Islamic principles that are evident to all Muslims. Saliently this is that God exists and we must both Love and Fear Him in a test of life that is based on achieving the maximum amount of moral action. We argue that through the use of moral calculus and the injection of moral principles into the nation-state there is political, economic and social progress towards the ideal."

A state is defined in terms of a set of institutions connected to a social group or groups by means of various contractual (de jure or de facto) agreements. It has become a centre of production and reproduction of violence and power over a geographical territory associated with a name, e.g. the UK or Iraq.

Analysis of history in simple terms in Islamic philosophy would outline a series of causes and effects in a networked chain necessarily extending back in time to reach the uncaused cause, God. God's existence is taken as a given or perhaps is inferred from empirical propositions, which are secrets that cannot be told directly to any non-believer, the reason for this a secret in itself.

From God's existence, one obtains an understanding of God's attributes, since God is known as His attributes. His attributes are uncontensiously defined as being love and strength, the All Merciful, the All Mighty. From this we obtain our relation with God, to Love Him and to Fear Him. Love of God implies love of what He has created, guards, guides and in the finality of this world- judges. Fear of angering God causes us to restrain and reduce damaging His creation, prominently and saliently, humanity. Loving God and His creation implies helping and enhancing His creation.

From this we can infer the meaning of life, for God has given the universe and its inhabitants a meaning. We call this meaning the engagement in moral action. From this we obtain the purpose of the state, since the state represents society it must draw its meaning from society. Society is composed of humans who have been contacted by God and commanded to engage in moral action, thus the purpose of society is to create the maximum opportunity for this objective and indeed this is obtained by society being moral as an emergent effect of individual morality. Since society's meaning is moral action then the state has as its core meaning, you might say core value, moral action. The state is presumed to have the ability to create structures of itself which influence and enhance the nation's ability to be at one with its purpose. Clearly action will involve things that are not moral action, but their central basis, their root, is moral action. Moral action is something that is undertaken that has an effect which can be judged to be good. We feel that the sacred texts put judgement of humanity more on the basis of what results from our action rather than what we intended to achieve. Manslaughter is still a crime even if it does not have the intentionality of murder. Islamic political theory as expounded here is a positive prescriptive framework.

"the Emperor's new Liberty"

We now turn to the competing contemporary framework for the state, that of the liberal democracy. In a descriptive rather than ideal sense, this is a sham, as is clear by the lack of voter turnout, apathy among the population, and endless political jockeying by competing powerful groups. However in its ideal it represents a significant challenge to Islamic political theory. Liberal theory gives boundaries for free action and just that. Society forms itself under internal dynamics which cannot be guided by great individuals because the central ethos is not to accept control. Without guidance humanity is lost, it is a stochastic system perhaps a random walk with drift tending towards ever more base desires and increasingly time compressed joys. Thus moral action is not upheld as the purpose of being. Society degenerates and with freedom blunting its weapons of mass attraction to goodness, cannot reproduce itself as a moral force. Elites start using hysteria to form consensus, but their lies create mistrust of them, thus power fades from the centre. The survival of the vacuous liberal society as a moral institution becomes jeopardised year by year and the economic becomes the core value that is held by all. The belief in freedom as a core value is an empty promise, since it does not by its nature prescribe what is good. In essence it is defined in liberal theory that all actions are good as long as they do not cause harm to another. This is the point of criticism or at least disjuncture with the Islamic political theory we have deduced above. The set of all good action does not correspond exactly to the set of all actions which do not harm another, though clearly there is some overlap. The disjuncture between Islam and Liberalism is that the nature of good action must be examined more closely. Liberalism is Lazy on this point. Liberalism also does not define the state's purpose which leads to, in the Despotic-Democracies of the existing Western nations, processes which we have outlined above resulting in continual degradation and degeneracy. This Qutbian-style argument, the approach of beginning one's quest for Islam from the existing state of the West, to look for progress by a critique of Liberal democracy, flows in a different direction to Qutb, since he himself was equally vacuous as Liberalism in terms of carefully and analytically defining the purpose of the state and the steps back from that which would have given his writings a more solid foundation, his arguments on social justice aside.

A pluralist Liberal would say that this argument that shows shortcomings of liberalism does not apply to her. This is because the pluralist says that society is a given (we would say by history) and freedom allows different elements of society to freely act as long as they do not harm others elements of society. We would not wish to go against useful ideas, indeed it is a historical fact that Islamic societies of the Medieval period operated a parallel judicial system for non-Muslims, effectively giving a kind of judicial devolution though not a political one. There is no disjuncture between pluralism and Islam in ideal, though in practice pluralism gives rise to pressure groups whose power takes over the legitimate population's desires and wishes. Without the call to moral action, the struggle for it internally and externally, all systems fall into the dust.

The problem of pluralism, which also applies to the pluralistic Islam we advocate, is that of Plato's ship. The ship can only go in one direction, thus government cannot aggregate contradiction and so consensus becomes difficult to obtain. There is the difference in language, model and values of different social groups which is the Habermasian argument of distorted communication stopping consensus formation. There is crucially the contradiction of progressive democratic consensual societies, i.e. debate must continue to obtain better solutions to problems but debate eliminates consensus on these solutions. An answer to this contradiction is for an elite to carry out the debate while the rest of the population simply obeys the elite, which is largely the model in Western democracy. The similarity of Shafi'I's elite of scholars determining Islamic rules which Muslims must obey and the Democratic West is a key point. We reject Western democracy as it is de jure, but in doing so we must also reject Shafi'I and what is generally termed the Shariah in favour of a reestablishment of God's rule in Muslim countries. The point on which we reject both these systems is that the elite become arrogant, unattached and unrepresentative of the population that they lead, which results in a legitimation crisis. Information flow between the population and the elite becomes problematic due to the lack of knowledge of how to aggregate preferences in such a way as to obtain consensus. This problem was outlined by Rousseau and lead him to the belief in small direct democracies as being the only sustainable and legitimate system. Of course there is an answer to the information flow aggregation problem in large nation-states. This is to expand the number of participants in the debate with a social norm that everyone must follow the law. More people engaged in the debate results in a nationwide discussion on the definition of moral action in our Islamic nation-state. This leads to a greater feeling of ownership of the law and leads to better laws due to the computational superiority of ever larger groups of people communicating with one another. The superiority of the ideas from this debate lead to people viewing them as legitimate, the ownership of these ideas by the people leads them to see these ideas as legitimate. Thus the deviation between law and action becomes small under the continual grand national debate.

Aggregation of people's ideas and policy preferences does not necessarily have to be accurate to obtain consensus, it must simply not be contested. There is necessarily no logical answer to the aggregation problem. Expanding the debate to more participants reduces macro disintegration of consensus (contestation by political groups) as well as micro disintegration (contestation by individuals) through deviation of action from law. The former is reduced by the superiority of ideas produced by all-inclusive national debate, while the latter is reduced by ownership of ideas by the people.

To obtain uncontested policy in Liberal democracy, the elite resorts to enhancing a vain media narrative that leads to a deviation from the moral, often in the form of apathy or perhaps in the form of unconditional acceptance such as ephemeral patriotism. The basis of these narratives is often lies or truths that leave out important information and evidence.

The Islamic approach to uncontested policy is based on argument using the truth, mutual respectful discussion by all under the direction of guidance from the greater persons. We outline below a general analytical approach for obtaining a ranking and prioritisation of policy options, which we call Moral Calculus. From Moral Calculus adequately estimated and discussed throughout society there is the production of communicative tools for obtaining consensus. We take it as natural law that humanity is attracted towards what it sees as good, thus if people discussed in truth what was the best course for society then there would be an eventual result of law and government action being driven towards moral action. This is the Islamic dialectic, a method of giving a degenerate society a higher moral purpose as undertaken by the Prophet (saw), and enshrined in the Qur'an, for achieving the purpose of the Islamic state (moral action) which causes society to become moral and achieve its purpose as set out by God. This rests on the forces of the moral being a substantial proportion of society and being vocal, integrated with society as well as ever engaged in reforming society and the self for the better (i.e. towards spreading the belief in moral action, both inwardly and outwardly). So the teaching and internalisation of moral calculus as well as its analytical development results in a bringing together of different belief systems, we suggest that religions of all societies would have in their intersection moral calculus for ranking choices, and so leads to consensus in a continual national debate of all persons. This leads to social and economic progress towards the ideal moral nation-state.

Natural law is defined and assumed as God's law, for God is the source of nature and all that there is. In all religious beliefs this is consensually defined as a common commandment for humanity to do moral action.

In the Liberal tradition, one may say that natural law, the consensus on what is good, is 'life, liberty and the pursuit of happiness'. But life is a given and we see no disjuncture between liberalism and Islamic political philosophy in this case, apart from that in Liberalism one has a life of liberty, which is the gift of an empty box. The pursuit of happiness reduces to degeneracy as society finds only base desire to follow as well as media magnified vane symbols. Fame becomes the frame around a picture that is only a frame in itself. The infinite regress and self-referential nature of fame- I exist as a celebrity because people know who I am (perhaps because others know me), a celebrity being someone who is known by many others, is symptomatic of the fetishtistic bottomless pit of Fire that liberal society has dug itself into. Moral action is the inverse of seeking fame. It places value where people positively affect others rather than being (in the case of fame) positively affected by others (in their knowing and valuing you).

Thus we conclude this section by noting that we have lifted the night niqab of the liberal nation-state that oppresses humanity and we release the world from the chains of ugly equality to allow them to find value in the moral value.

"Give me martyrdom or give me death"

Moral Calculus

Defending liberty against our reproaches would suggest that there is little guidance on how choices are made. Clearly if one simply leaves it to the democratic consensus in this Islamic political philosophic theory then one is simply replacing vacuous liberty with a vacuum under the name of Islam.

To avoid this contention we outline moral calculus, a method which gives an analytical framework for differentiating between different actions in order to find the moral ideal.

The problem of aggregating preferences outlined above as well as the Habermasian distorted communication issue and the essential tension in debate to achieve consensus is soothed by this analytical approach since a common standard for assessing of policy options is proposed.

Below are defined different effect functions for present, future and afterlife:

$T(0)$ = present
$T(1)$ = future
$T(2)$ = afterlife

A weighted index is created with weights; $c>b>a$:

$A \times T(0) + B \times T(1) + C \times T(2)$

The exact configuration of the weights depends on one's attitude to uncertainty. This must be distinguished from risk as there is no certainty of any of the outcomes occurring. Risk and thus the computation of expected probability implies that on average the outcome is known, if the outcomes were to be run and re-run many times over. Uncertainty is where we do not have expected probabilities and to compute them would be misleading. One cannot have several goes at moral action at those junctures outlined in moral calculus. Clearly there is a further issue of the expected probability of success of the choice, which needs some assignment of probability to the index. This can be computed from historical information and modelling of the issue in question. One can have several tries at different choices so there is the prospect of using expected probability across the entire result but there is always a fundamental uncertainty as to whether the result of the afterlife is worth the cost in the present and future.

From this data on choices, perhaps similar to the method suggested by Ross Perot in regard to democratic involvement in budgetary decisions of US Federal Government, the population can be persuaded by different choices and give feedback for more elucidation, disagreements with calculation and assumptions, suggestions of new choices and in the final analysis, decisions on where they stand, possibly including why they believe in a particular choice over another.

All things are only made superior if they are placed alongside something else, it is the necessary nature of the greater than sign in logic that there are at least two elements being compared as it is in language for a proposition involving the words "greater than". Heaven needs Hell. Hell needs Heaven. So Moral Calculus needs its Hell, something to compare itself with for legitimacy. We use Cost Benefit analysis for this. The principle difference between cost benefit analysis and Moral calculus is that an afterlife is added in the latter. However an inequality is assumed in Moral Calculus between the greater and the lesser humans, in favour of the lesser. This point is found through the contradiction we outline below in Cost Benefit Analysis.

Secular Liberal Cost Benefit analysis proceeds from an assumption which is considered objective of equality between different people's levels of happiness adduced by some measure such as money. In this method one adds up the benefits to all people in the present and future and take away the costs for judging between policy options. There are many subsidiary issues in cost-benefit analysis but it is essentially compressing happiness in society by established metrics in the literature of economics in present and future with the assumption that there is no afterlife. However consider a policy of reallocating assets from rich to poor people. Under cost benefit analysis each person's happiness is weighted equally so a reallocation leads to no net gain. This is a subjective principle, many societies in antiquity would have rated the sovereign as having greater weight on their happiness than the rest of the population. Liberalism brought in the equality of weighting to all people's happiness. But this leads us to a contradiction, a paradox at least, that the assumption of equality would make us judge against reducing economic inequality. One simply cannot morally say that the giving of an additional pound to a rich woman affects their happiness the same as an additional pound to a poor woman, it is as repugnant as it is wrong. A counter argument given to me concerning this point is that one is making a value judgement in giving more worth to the poor than the rich. But equality is itself a value judgement, it is small 't' truth of the Liberal society that has been cemented in history for so long that people do not criticise it. Both judgements therefore are equal in their subjective validity. As one can summarise Descartes' argument of one not being to deduce the existence of the world since it could all be an illusion of the devil's making, one cannot be necessarily objective. All truths and Truths are intersubjective realities, consensus' which gives us hope for the consensus centred morally active Islamic nation-state.

The issue of atonement for sin.

Related to the issue of Justice, which is the punishment of the sinner who has wronged another by an external party most possibly the state, though not necessarily, is the issue of atonement for sin, which is where the sinner punishes himself perhaps under the direction and judgement of the state's institutions or perhaps reduces harm / increases happiness to people who they have wronged, even if such deeds are only symbolic. To obtain a moral course one is not just looking for the best outcome for humanity as computed above in 'next and this world' utilitarian terms, but also with regard to making up for and repairing the damage one has caused. The exact approach for this depends on the sin but a moral society must make public available information on strategies for atonement of sin in parallel to its judicial system. This information may be produced by society in its discussions. Atonement is not just for individuals but also for nations and social identities.

The Morally competitive market

The definition in society and state of moral action being the purpose of life, nation and state, leads to competition among people through the tennis effect (also called the revenge effect) for control of moral assets. The economic (money), political (institutional effect and structure) and social assets (social institution formation and reproduction) are sought after and are turned into moral assets through their use for achieving moral action.

This is analogous to profit maximisation in economic theory. Since profit maximisation leads to optimal allocations for society in economic terms of value, moral competition leads to optimal allocations for society in moral terms of value. The economic argument says that a person following their Earthly drives for happiness leads to the maximum happiness for all, so if a person is defined as finding their happiness in the identity of the moral with action then the result is analogously that the most moral outcome is chosen and results. The identification by economists of economic optimality leading to social optimality sidesteps the reallocation of assets for moral purposes, the implication being that greater degrees of equality may be superior morally to inequality of certain orders of magnitude.

Realisation of the Moral High Ground, the choices which are most good in comparison to other political groups, as a political tool for attaining attraction and support for one's political group, leads to political elites jockeying for position for the more moral course and policy. The individual's desire to obtain the best choices under moral calculus leads them to a rush towards moral action. The business' desire to add value for its owners leads them to be pressured by individuals' value of moral action to themselves engage in obtaining the moral high ground among their competitors.

We expand our earlier point that moral action leads to superior results morally speaking than under the assumptions of Liberal democratic capitalism. Consider the Edgeworth Box. This secular model of a 2 person economy where any given allocation of resources leads to Pareto Optimal results necessarily if people trade two different goods. Pareto Optimality is where there is no better allocation without making someone else worse off. This is shown to be where the marginal rate of substitution between goods is equal for both parties. The Morally competitive market is where one adds in the prospect of Heaven as a reward for moral action. Consider a simplification of the Edgeworth Box to the allocation between two parties who make up the economy of 1 good. We shall call this an Edgeworth line which is defined as having length 1 as a simplification, the length being the total amount of the goods in the economy. A moral action is confined in this analysis to being the giving in charity from the rich to the poor. $X1$ is the amount of the good that person 1 has and $x2$ is the amount of the good that person 2 has. The algorithm for moral action is that if $x1 > x2$ then person 1 is richer than person 2 so person 1 can increase their utility in the afterlife by reallocating resources to the poorer person. This algorithm is in the other way around if person 2 is richer than person 1. Thus where $x1$ equals $x2$ there is an equilibrium and no further change in state can occur. Since $x2 = (1 - x1)$ then equilibrium is $x1 = 1 - x1$ which gives the result $x1 = ½ = x2$. Thus equality is the tendency of moral action in allocation of resources. The Edgeworth Box is a con since it obfuscates the distribution of resources problem with the decision to maximise between two goods. Since the choice is limited to the two goods the question of the income distribution is overlooked.

As a digression we give the economist who reads this a subtle choice that may lead them to accept our fundamental premise, that God exists. The market is often shown through General Competitive Equilibrium Analysis (GCE) to be the optimal allocator of resources by economists. But Dinwiddy has shown that if the firm is replaced by the state in this analysis then the state is shown to be the optimal allocator of resources. One can show that this is entirely incorrect for both firm and state by recourse to the argument that demolishes the ontological argument for God's existence. This is where man is assumed to exist but is considered imperfect. God is perfect. Since perfection intersects the characteristics of imperfection then since man exists, God exists. However the counter argument to this is that an imaginary perfect island is put in the argument in place of God with the result that something that is deduced to exist which is a contradiction with the definition of an imaginary island. If one put an imaginary firm in place of the firm of general equilibrium analysis then we come to the same answer, something that does not exist is the best allocator of resources. Coming back to the ontological argument, if one wishes to say that with GCE, that either the capitalist system or command economy is the perfect allocator of resources, then one must accept the ontological argument for God is true, since one has to disregard the imaginary agent counter argument by coming up with some reason for its invalidity. Therefore the economist who believes in GCE, whether they are from the left or right, must accept the ontological argument for God's existence, which brings them to the propositions put forward at the start of this essay.

In conclusion, the moral drive is a viable allocator of resources for the purpose of reproducing the nation-state and enhancing itself and humanity as a whole. The economist may disagree with us by saying that the moral imperative is weaker than the economic, but he comes from the secular Western democracy which has degenerated from its historical moral purpose and seeks to replace moral purpose at the heart of every society in the world through Globalisation. This is the fight back and we shall see which course wins in the end.

> *"the battle for the soul of humanity begins here"*

16. Truth, Democracy and Statistics

David Cameron, UK Conservative Leader outlined an issue on his weblog about the problem of aggregating people's comments and views for use by the representative politician. Clearly one answer to this is the referendum, a simple question that is passed if a majority agree with it. Opinion polls are also similar simple means of aggregation. But their drawback is that in compressing the information that is available to the researcher on the opinions of a democracy, there is signal degradation, that is one does not account for the various nuances and shades of belief. The question can be created through analysis of conversation trees to put the voters into a situation where they agree in majority with the person who sets the question.

Thus what is required for research is to create statistical means whereby one can aggregate loosely structured sentences together from everyone in the debate of a nation-state to provide a spectrum of opinion rather than a boolean true or false result of an opinion poll. Statistics use the language of numbers so this is a difficult task, but what might be needed is an advance in the understanding sentence structures that lead to an aggregated sentence. The other way is to create indices of belief that aggregate the sentences produced in a debate to give numerical output, perhaps a policy matrix, where each dimension is a different policy direction.

The use of the term statistics as being the tool of solving the aggregation problem in democracy is misleading however, as one could construct the 'complete' sentence which encompassed the entire debate on a subject. Clearly this would be by the definition of a debate (a clashing of contrary arguments) an incoherent sentence, so this is unsatisfactory. Another approach is to draw a diagram with each of the contrary opinions against each other. To be certain, as we increase the numbers of people in a debate this will quickly be difficult to contain clearly in a simple diagram.

Another answer is for people to self select their closeness to various existing arguments and opinions so that a policy matrix can be built up easily. This has the drawback of subjectivity and political bias.

An example of a policy matrix:
```
      1           2           3           4
{pro war     anti war    anti war    pro war  }
{anti terror anti terror pro terror  pro terror}   diagram A
```

Diagram A shows an example of a 4 x 2 policy matrix. Contained here are a number of different opinions expressed by a group of hypothetical citizens. Citizen 1, whose views are given in column 1, is for the war on terror but against terrorism. Citizen 2 is against the war and against terrorism. These are archetypal mutually exclusive views and we call them policy vectors. They are different and cannot be aggregated. Many people will have opinions in each of these archetypes. A policy matrix could thus contain all the different variations in thought and be simplified by hand in small samples or through analysis using a computer to obtain a first reduction, that is where policy vectors which are exactly the same are reduced to the number of identical policy vectors. So if there are 10 people who are anti-war and anti-terror and 2 people who are pro-war and anti-terror then the policy matrix after first reduction is (2, 10). A second reduction can be created whereby similar viewpoints are put together using fuzzy logic or some similar technique.

Therefore what may be an n dimensional policy matrix (where n is the number of citizens with views in a debate) becomes after second reduction possibly manageable enough for a representative politician to make sense of after some study. Over time it is likely that one will find recurring themes.

17. A justification of a plan to end poverty through alternative Economic Theory

The idea: end world poverty by raising wealth in the economy. We suggest a 0.5% Tobin tax that will raise a projected £1.25 trillion per year. This money is used to employ people in developing countries to build primarily houses and other assets which are then given to the poor. Careful analysis should provide the exact amount of houses to be built so as not to create oversupply. The stimulus of the aid package should circulate in the poor economies raising house and other asset prices as well as stimulating investment in productive activity. This raises the wealth in the poor countries which makes them have higher GDP growth. We argue that raising wealth is the key way to facilitate the market. Our analysis shows that developed countries will eventually reach a maximum GDP which they cannot go ahead without redistributing wealth to LDCs. We argue that building houses is a means to amplify aid given to developing countries, since houses go up in value.

We take concepts from fluid mechanics (sinks and sources) to represent the flow of money in an economy, the insight being that the economy is best represented as the dynamic system of a flow of water moving round points a space which represents different people in the economy. We use insight expressed in language rather than the so called rigorous approach of contemporary economics, which we feel does not achieve truth over time since it is limited in terms of the kinds of systems and processes it can express through mathematics. This is strictly speaking political economy in the vein of the classical thinkers such as Malthus and Adam Smith. These thinkers would identify systems and processes and think about likely scenarios that would be produced.

Bank lending goes to the rich, so make the poor rich.

The principal of banking as an institution is to lend more money to those with more assets. In developing countries there are not many assets therefore there is less lending. More lending raises economic growth. Since a bank is a sink, that is it draws in much of the money in an economy like a black hole, there will be low growth since money will not be recycled to other people. There will be a one way flow of money towards lenders. By creating assets like houses as our plan suggests, the bank is turned from a sink of money to a source, that is a positive contributor to the economy. By making houses for many poor people, more lending is available for business owned by the poor. Thus the poor have a greater chance of becoming rich. This is like an inversion of microcredit, which involves lending to the poorest in small amounts. By raising the amount of wealth of the poor and then letting the market lend large sums to them to create more wealth, a faster move out of poverty occurs overall.

An argument against this is that such a process was undertaken by banks in the 2007 credit crisis in America. Here banks would excessively lend money to low income/ uncertain income households based on their existing assets. We must see that in this case they raised the amount of liabilities for the poor, while we suggest raising the amount of assets owned by the poor. What this event does make clear is that lending must be a relationship between a bank who assesses the feasibility of the reason a borrower wants funds for.

Essential to the approach is to make sure that borrowed funds are put into value adding activities, such as business and learning, as opposed to fuelling a consumption bubble.

The depression inducing effects of debt repayments from LDCs.

Many developing countries' governments have high levels of debt. There seems to be large amounts of particularly foreign denominated debt held by governments in these nations. We suggest that the reason for this may be a feedback compounding process that raises the level of foreign denominated debt held over time very quickly.

The process is as follows; foreign debt is taken which goes up by its interest rate. As the debt interest is paid, the exchange rate devalues, due to the massive exchange of money required to pay the debt interest off. This puts the balance of payments into deficit (given the fact that many factors such as poor marketing and poor quality products lead the demand curve for LDCs to be flat) which itself must be financed by debt, which in turn increases the interest payments. Overall the debt increases taking an ever larger part of the state's expenditure and leads to default eventually. This process is increased by compounding of the various flows. According to Keynes, money flowing out of the economy will reduce GDP.

The Prebisch Singer thesis states that developing countries exchange rates have been devaluing. Our above analysis would give the reason for this as the massive outflow of funds to pay back debt as the reason for the pressure on exchange rates. Thus what is called for is a reversal of this with £1.25 trillion being pumped into developing countries' economies every year. This would benefit developed countries because it would reduce the incidence of debt crises and defaults.

Inflation and assets

Inflation is not a reality. It is an imposed idealisation put upon data to reduce the primacy of money. Money is what is moving throughout an economy in a feedback process, moving from person to person, stimulating them into activity that is useful for others. Inflation, given by an average basket of goods does show a phenomena of price feedback, that is prices that depend on other prices, but it is an overstated problem. For example, in harsh times people will switch consumption to cheaper goods, goods which may be of a lower quality. Thus the uncertainty of knowing the right basket of goods to calculate inflation is apparent.

Thus we can see that the difference between real and non-real growth is near impossible to calculate. Thus we see the primacy of money in an economy. When we unlock ourselves from the inflationary chains we see that things like assets become deeply important for the economy. Looking at inflation adjusted income we would see asset rises as a decline in the growth of the economy. But rather they are the source of development. The myriad channels in which assets raise the amount of money in the economy combined with the fact that asset prices, while increased by the amount of money that goes into the asset market, can go much higher than the total amount of money in the economy. This is because only a small proportion of assets are traded at any one time. Thus most of the assets are held in expectation of capital growth or because they have a useful cultural value, like houses.

Market size and demand

The maximum market size of any product is assumed to be finite. A household would only have 1 washing machine, 1 or 2 cars, 1 microwave oven. Thus a policy that caused income to become more evenly distributed would result in greater demand overall. Keynes noted a similar outcome but through a different process. He stated that the proportion of income consumed declines as income rises. This is perhaps given some credibility by our finite market size argument.

This implies that a policy to make the poor in the world richer would increase the size of the global economy, making everyone better off. This is because the total market size would increase because more people would be able to demand goods. Developed as well as developing countries would benefit.

Memetic theory of house prices

A meme is a basic unit of cultural information. It can be anything, any message sent from one person to another. The y spread much like a virus until they reach the whole of society and form a consensus. Their dynamics are highly variable and unpredictable though consensus can hold for long periods of time. In the housing market, memes propagate of the overall state of the market. System wide memes saying whether the market is thriving or in recession spread. At times the housing market is in boom, thus the boom meme is dominant. At other times it is the slump meme that forms the consensus. A criticism of the our plan to build houses is that it would create a surplus of houses and thus reduce the average house price. Our contention is that the reason why house prices go up is a memetic phenomena. They go up because the consensus is that house prices will go up. The stimulus package of construction suggested by our campaign would create the expectations of house price rises.

In short houses go up in value because people believe that they are going up. While demand and supply are key processes in the memetic system, the belief that something is valued at a certain amount is something that is transmitted throughout the network of people. Mania's and panics in asset markets talked about by Kindleberger are more thoroughly analysed as memetic phenomena.

Value

Goods are given value, that is the amount of money someone will pay for them, through the creation of brand names. Some brand names are from small businesses which create goodwill from their interaction with customers. Corporate brand names come from the interaction with society through advertising and Corporate Social Responsibility.

Before capitalism or the free market economy there is no value in society. As capitalism progresses new ideas are created for products, archetypes of the goods that are produced. Historically changing mechanisms come about for the creation of new archetypes and the attachment of value to them by society.

Thus is places like Africa many things are not given much value. As an economy develops and people's incomes rise, value rises due to the pressure on prices of goods and services produced by firms. This raises the total amount of GDP, in essence 'value added', thus growth occurs. But this process needs a rising amount of money in the economy. The source of this money would be the increase in asset wealth produced by the plan we have given.

Feedback in the asset based free market economy

We look at feedback in the spending and investment as well as the growth of assets which are hypothesised to not take money from the economy.

Of £1 that is earned by a worker, 80p is spent on consumption. This cycles back into another persons earnings which increases the GDP of the economy to £1.80. This process continues until the earning is 0p.

Of the £1 earned by the first worker, 20p is invested in assets. This asset can go up or go down. If the asset doubles to 40p then the economic wealth of the society has doubled. No new money has been injected into the economy when the asset goes up in value but the wealth of the economy has doubled. Our proposed plan relies on building assets, in this case houses, that raise the wealth of the economy and thus impact on economic growth. When the asset is sold or a loan is secured on it, the worker can spend or invest more growing the economy.

As poor people would be employed to build the houses in our campaign (see Home page) they would spend much of the money they earn. This moves money moves on to the people from whom they bought goods. These people spend their money so money moves to others and so on. In this way more activity is created by injections of money into the economy. This feedback process, whereby an injection of money flows through the economy in transactions through many people making them engage in activity and also helping to fund investment and thus longer term activity is the essence of why the free market economy works so well. The problem with the free market economy is that there are sinks (as in a dynamic system) where most money flows towards without being recycled in the economy. One of the reasons why there are sinks is because many people do not have much money thus there is a lessening of economic activity due to poverty. This is the situation we see in developing countries.

Figure 1.0 shows a notional tree of money flowing between individuals. Each circle represents a person and the number shows the amount of money they have. The arrow shows the direction of consumption in other words the flow of money from one node to another. Each movement of money takes place in a single time period so the diagram shows 3 distinct time periods.

In time=0, the top tier node has £10. This node spends all their money on products from the two nodes beneath it, each of whom receive £5. Activity of those nodes in producing products has been increased. In time=1 the second tier nodes spend all their money on two other nodes each, though one node in the centre is a sink and receives money from many nodes and thus ends up having more money. Assuming that there are 3 time periods in a year, national income is £30 though money supply is £10. What we can see is that the reason why capitalism works so well is because of the feedback effect of money flowing through the society and stimulating people into activity.

Another point to make from this analysis is that the theory that raising money supply creates inflation is not necessarily true. Money simply flows in the economy and it is unlocked from the generation of price feedback (our subdivision of inflation as a concept) by our argument given above. In fact this analysis is similar to the quantity theory of money, but the novel feature that helps us is the analysis of money flow into different people in the economy and without linking inflation into the system. Keynes also touched on the concept of the flow of money but he subdivided the economy into firms and households, which we believe to not be general enough to give us true insight and also does not give a direct representation of the economy. The point of this kind of analysis is that it allows us to make a simple argument. If the amount of money in an economy is increased then national income increases, though how long this can occur will depend on how many and how powerful sinks are.

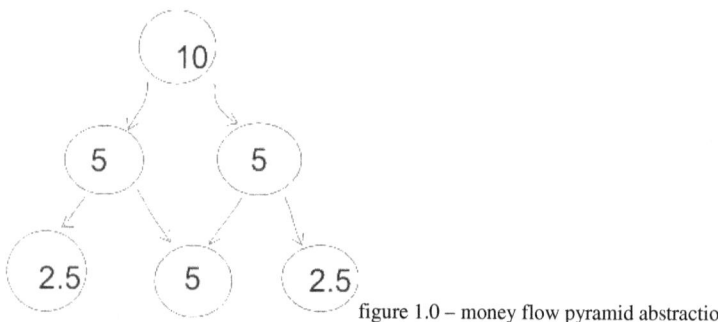

figure 1.0 – money flow pyramid abstraction

We can generalise this approach to representing money flow in the economy with a matrix of agents where each element of the matrix represents the bank account of each agent (Agent matrix). Another matrix determines the percentage of money that flows (spending) to each agent from each agent (transformation matrix, $T(t(i), t(j))$ where $1 > t(i), t(j) > 0$). The agent matrix is multiplied by the transformation matrix repeatedly each period. What is noticeable is that while the bank accounts of each matrix goes up or down, the overall level of money in the economy has not changed. Money will tend to flow into some agents who are sinks, for example owners of large amounts of assets such as banks or supermarket chains. National income is given by the sum of many agents income in a period of time, there being many transactions in any period.

If assets are created for the poorer agents then lending can occur from the rich to them thus circulating money throughout the economy.

Sinks can be represented in this formulation as agents which have many if not all other agents spending much of their money on them. Houses are a sink in fact all assets are, but when they draw money towards them they become larger in value thus creating conditions whereby there is an outflow of money from houses into the economy. Thus tackling poverty through building assets is a viable technique to amplify aid flows.

Assets price growth

The essential property of assets is that they can grow to very high amounts, well out of proportion to the amount of money in an economy. The reason why is because only a small part of the total amount of assets in an economy are traded. The money that supports asset price growth is thus concentrated, so a boost to the economy can raise asset prices to very high levels. This unplugs sinks like banks and gets them to recirculate their money to people in society. The recipients of these loans will have a higher chance of creating new assets and flows of money if they start up larger and better businesses. Thus the economy grows by very high rates with wide dispersion of assets.

Housing Wealth

Some would argue that raising the amount of houses in poor countries would reduce their average price. This is a crude demand curve analysis. However, demand shifts up when there is a rise in wealth. Furthermore building large amounts of houses as in our plan raises and redistributes the total housing wealth which is average price times number of houses. This would have an impact on the economy even if prices were slow to increase.

18. Perfect Competition, a critical disjuncture with the conventional wisdom

Perfect competition is the supposed outcome of a number of assumptions regarding capitalism. Any argument can be analysed at its core, that is the important mechanisms involved in producing the outcome it suggests. While many have criticised perfect competition through the departure of reality from its strict assumptions, we say one should use the eye of reason to understand what exactly perfect competition theory is talking about and why this is not true, in order to come up with a considered and powerful critique of this.

Perfect competition suggests that firms are price takers, the market determines the price they set. The decision maker in the firm can only affect the cost structure according to this theory by determining the amount it will sell. As such it is suggested then that the long run outcome is that firms will produce a quantity and sell it entirely up to the point where marginal cost crosses average cost. Marginal cost can be seen loosely as variable cost, the unit cost for 1 more unit, without an apportionment of fixed costs to this. Average cost includes fixed costs and thus is initially drawn as downward sloping due to economies of scale.

The reason why the perfect competition model is beyond repair is because the flow of information, power of decision makers and outcome in terms of sales and cost structure is not accurately depicted. A firm may put much effort into forecasting sales but it seems quite likely that such forecasts have a significant margin of error. A simple reason for this is that sales will depend, among other things, on how much is produced by all competing firms. Thus each firm in the market needs to have a model of each other firm's sales forecast in order to create a sales forecast. Thus Gödel's Theorem would tell us that this kind of self-referential system cannot be put into mathematics or logic. Thus there can be no complete model of sales forecasts for either the individual firm or for the market. In reality, firms use heuristic analysis, look at past trends, economic indicators and market research to come to a number for sales forecasts. As a result firms are often observed to be sales maximisers, looking to increase market share above all else.

A significant advance in the theory of supply could be made should a thorough analysis of the mechanism for sales forecasts to be made and developed over time as is actually used by firms.

Since there is no a priori way of knowing ones sales, the amount produced, given a lag between when goods are made and goods are sold, means that the average cost curve does not exist when the firm is making the decision as to the quantity to produce. Thus the disorganisation of capitalism can lead to overproduction or undersupply, simply from the aspect of the decisions a firm makes. Since the firm does not have an average cost curve, as it could invest in machinery but then find it can't sell a single unit, or it may under invest and perhaps run out of stock. This latter result is not a long term problem given sustained sales growth as the firm can always invest in new machinery later. A firm may want to trade at levels which are most profitable for it, but there is no necessity of a firm making any sales. Customers in capitalism have a certain freedom of choice.

A second problem is the addition of debt and interest repayments on capital as well as on costs for running the business. The structure of the average cost curve means that a firm in the perfect competition model must have Seers and Mystics with the ability to see clearly into the future in order to be able to structure its financing structure with the production process and market demand. As central banks alter interest rates, often depending on the pricing decisions of the market/collection of competing firms, there is clearly an additional macroeconomic area necessary for inclusion into the model.

A third and most obvious point is that firms set the price of a product. This is evident from even the most casual interaction with business. The idea that a firm may not be able to do this because of market pressure due to the ability of consumers to switch to a different product actually causes large problems and is a possible mechanism for the cause of recessions or slow growth. Many firms in reality are oligopolies. They optimise with respect to risk and profit to stabilise market prices and reduce competition, as can be seen by understanding just what business strategy theory produces as a norm (Michael Porter, Competitive Strategy).

In summary the model of perfect competition suggests that firms will produce up to the point where price=marginal cost=average cost. Since sales cannot be forecast by Gödel's theorem due to a self-referentiality in a true sales forecast model of firms, the firm cannot know a priori its average cost curve. Thus they cannot set the amount of production therefore the perfect competition model breaks down. A few simple observations show that a firm has different characteristics to the perfect competition model of the firm; in terms of not knowing its sales, but being able to set a price at whatever it wishes. Thus we conclude that perfect competition is a misleading model and that accurate research to develop this key area of macroeconomic analysis must involve a greater degree of accuracy and empirical rigour based on observing and identifying the key tendencies of the economy and then relating it to other areas in a sense seeing everything as it is.

As an alternative to perfect competition we see from looking at different business' that the key force of their strategy is to create economic rents or restriction in supply. For example, the PC industry has no patent on the overall technology so rivalry leads to a great reduction in profits and therefore the business has become commoditised. On the other hand the existence of a patent on the microprocessor CPU such as for Intel's chip leads to large rents for this company. From the stand point of the idea map that will generate the tendency of behaviour of business managers we can look at Michael Porter's book on Strategy. Here he essentially turns the perfect competition model on its head and essentially prescribes to business managers to do everything they can to avoid competition through building up capabilities. Here we see that business' concept of value adding and the economic concept of value, surplus or economic rent is essentially similar if not actually approaching exactly the same concept from different academic methodologies. Thus we have an alternative to perfect competition, a rent seeking model of firms which aim to reduce competition and create rents through their capabilities. Thus there is no concept of efficiency and Pareto Optimality or the necessary superiority of free market based capitalism is not conclusively held. Consider the high rates of productivity of China compared to other nations in the late 1990s and early 21st Century. This country has a large state sector thus market efficiency cannot be empirically held as a universal law given these high levels of productivity. On the other hand, looking at productivity as value added growth, in other words the development of successful rent seeking by firms, leads to one seeing a reason why China has had much higher levels of productivity growth than say India or Africa.

There is also the demand creating effects of firms which involves linking their product into the idea map of the society they serve, thus culture is altered by capitalism, though this is also subject to dynamics.

19. A Centre to a Circle

A circle is a beautiful object. Its perfection through symmetry holds the eye. Analysis of the circle shows an edge of infinite sides and a centre around which all points are equally distributed.

So too is the circle of mankind, Liberalism. The centre is the will of the points around the circle, and if any point should move, all must move to maintain the circle's integrity as an object. Each point is equally near and far from the centre. The linked chain of each point, were one to follow a path from one to another, is infinite. This is the Liberal Aesthetic.

As a driver for social change in the Colonial powers of the West, it must not be underestimated. The analogy is of the power of sovereign, essentially the unchecked nebulous creature that is the centre of the circle as well as the government, the nation, the state of existence imbued with the desires of the people. In short, democracy in ideal. This must be distinguished from democrazy, the existing Liberal reality (which we call Liberality), where checked power is checked by itself and is in an endless loop among itself, deaf to the cry of progress, the wail of the suffering of mankind.

Each point of the edge of the circle is an individual. Its power to affect the state is given by its distance from the centre. All radii are equal. Thus the Liberal Aesthetic demands that each one may affect the centre (government) equally.

Marx extended the Liberal Aesthetic to redefine the centre as the economic reality, economic power, control of production. The tension between laissez-faire economics and Marxism is really a contradiction within the Liberal Aesthetic itself.

Take the analogy further and one sees that each point is related in position to each other and must maintain its relative position to the other points to keep the circle in existence. Should a member of society deviate from its position from the centre then all members of society should also move their position. Since position is power, that is the ability to exercise ones influence on the universal will of the centre, all must restrain or enhance themselves equally in the ability to exercise influence in response to the movement of another. Society may decide that people's power to influence the centre through violence, coup d'etats, riots, are not acceptable. But all must move away from this for the Liberal Aesthetic to be maintained. A particular person may become highly influential as a result of control of information. This particular person then becomes part of the centre which all are considered to have the right to influence equally.

Consider the growth of society and the expansion of diameter of the circle to accommodate more individuals. As society grows, each person's voice becomes drowned out by the others. The centre becomes arrogant and removed. The circle collapses away through apathy and corruption. The Liberal Aesthetic dies and we are only left with a historical ruin, a stone circle whose meaning is lost in history.

On the purpose of social science and the methodology to produce progress

Montesquieu takes law to be relational issuing from the nature of things. In other words a law is a relation from structure. We have untrue laws, for example, Newtonian mechanics does not work for very small particles. We have discussed in other works that social science is chiefly about information compression. One person has eggs in the morning, another has cereal, another has niari and pouri. We can compress this sociological information and talk of people having a meal called "breakfast". Similarly the study of institutions can be seen as compression of the data into smaller packets of data; class, family, tribe. To some extent information compression as a goal of social science is the analogue of laws in natural sciences. It is pleasing to the heart of a social scientist to talk about the subject of society without recourse to a universal, grand narrative of Truth. Thank postmodernism. But social science needs a goal to organise itself and impose a centre around which the members of it can organise. A common code, a language structure, is required to be part of the centre. These kinds of goals, one might say codes/language structures form a nexus with the social relation and structure of an academic discipline and impose a trajectory on its debates.

In economics we see a lost fleet in pea soup fog lurching from one great tidal wave to another. This is an example of a methodological state and social structure of economists that has interacted to produce rampant nonsense for at least a century. Even through adoption of important and intelligent ideas from other sciences, the ideological tendency has been to be destructive and misleading answers to questions which currently leaves our world in problematic situations. An elite of economists have produced methodological goals and codes such as "rigorous analysis" and a plethora of mathematical objects and artifacts to mislead the state's members as to the nature of the economy. Essentially the strategy has been to block or perhaps funnel all acceptable analysis towards difficult mathematical techniques which are held as truths. In this way dissent from the orthodoxy of pro-capitalist ideology is contained and destroyed. Whilst this may have issued from the social tensions in wider society through the 20th Century, it clearly has left the capitalist system without chart, compass or navigator, though still captain and crew.

We see that the term "rigorous analysis" is a keyword in the methodological structure of economists, and it means the use of analytical methods involving mathematics. It effectively blocks economists from non-mathematical criticisms. Since the development of new mathematical structures is slower than the development of discourse, it is easier for economists to maintain the central narrative of economics; business is good, state is bad. Clearly though this has the downside of economists not knowing what to do when business is *not* good.

We use no sleight of hand in openly explaining that "information compression" is our suggestion as a keyword for thinking about the kinds of methodological structures needed for a successful progressive social science. However, unlike "rigorous analysis" it is not meant to steer the discipline towards a political agenda that has not even been thought through. Thus the keyword "rigorous analysis" is a conversation tree blocking strategy to maintain a small easily controlled elite of academics involved in the production of economic knowledge.

The process we believe the repetition of "information compression" will have on the development of social science is a gradual mapping and carving up of the society into overlapping categories. Clearly it is beneficial to compress information since this is easier to communicate. In this there is a political agenda, one of democratisation of social science, whereby simple ideas are promoted and spread widely through society so that it may be fulfilled by greater understanding of itself. The other side of the coin is that an elevation of the simple, in the sense of being easily communicated, leads to a widening of the number of people who can be involved in creating these ideas.

The third reason for using information compression is because this is an abstraction of what many great social scientists have done especially in respect of understanding society through its units of analysis, which are termed institutions. A class is many workers, a family is many households, a nation is many citizens.

The fourth outcome is the emphasis on subjective recognition of objective components of the social world. The mind puts the pieces of light together from a chair that it looks at and calls it a chair, rather than piece of light 001, 002, 003, etc. So too we feel that the mind can capably recognise objects in society.

An aside to the point of "information compression" is the downside risk of it. Shannon would tell us that information compression leads to signal degradation, that is loss of information. Thus we sacrifice heterogeneity in our work, though clearly there is a place for such approaches in social science to balance and eventually synthesise with the main body of work.

Coming back to information compression we suggest that this be used to create the units of analysis for social science. From here we need to organise these units into systems. This is where different units interact. Also we need to look at subsystems, that is where the components of the units interact. We can look at historical trajectories and debate counterfactuals to create hypothesis' about these systems. We can do comparative ex post experiments from looking at broadly similar yet slightly different systems to test some of these hypothesis' as well as create more of them. Thus this is the empirical element of the social scientist social structure.

At the same time a philosophical development is needed. This is to clarify what we are doing, what objective we have in mind and bringing together different strands of social science to see how coherent they are with each other. In other words there is philosophy as a coordinating mechanism in the social structure of social sciences.

A third element of the social scientist social structure is the development of "complexity analysis", that is the understanding of complex systems. Whilst physics understands individual atoms it does not understand the outcome of many bodies interacting in any deterministic (non-probabilistic) sense. Thought experiments and simulation are possible ways of going forward with this bottleneck in the social science methodological complex we are discussing.

With all three elements; an empirical democratic social science, a managerial philosophy of social science and a complexity and complex systems social science, we believe social science will be able to produce far more progressive and effective answers.

Just as from a circle, an infinity of equal radii are formed, so from this Tripartite system of disciplines in social science one can see a widening of the subject in terms of both membership and total number of ideas. More ideas are created but with greater skills developed in information compression, these ideas can become synthesised in the sense that the most convincing aspects of them are recognised. Certainly we are more likely to find the truth if we have more goes at the game of science. But it is highly likely that the downside risk for this approach is that we never really know which idea is correct. Thus we increase the chance of getting to the truth with the extra baggage of doubt. The benefit though is that we will have created in social science a common language from reason that can be diffused throughout society for which to give a centre much as law is at the centre of a court room. Therefore Liberality is dead. Long live Liberalism.

20. Anti-Americanism in British Society

We propose to study the rise of anti-Americanism (AA) in the UK. The social groups this sentiment is divided among are Muslims, Christians, The Left, The Media, Politicians, The Right. We also look at the sources of Muslim's in Britain's more radical understanding of the world like through a consideration of Osama Bin Laden's statements.

We propose to use data from publications by elements of these groups to elucidate the themes of AA. The thesis is that anti-Americanism is the UK's alcoholic lust for a dream world. The cure for this is the focus of our analysis. The prospect of hate that originates from AA is disturbing and possibly destabilising.

Methodology

We outline a few possible methodologies, that is algorithms and rules of seeking knowledge, here. At the core of our methodology is to create models of behaviour and use this to create a narrative for analysis. Our other element is perception, the ability of the human brain to recognise the object in question like recognising a face.

We can take narratives of history and abstract mechanisms that occur in it. This is essentially information compression, that is making a big narrative into a small model. From this we can find policy suggestions. We can also synthesise models and concepts from theories that are the information compression of historical narratives, such as Marx.

We can create models from stylised facts, that is reasoning from assumptions about the underlying structures that define an object of interest. This is done in economics and also physics.

We can take a critical realist approach, that is to take events and suggest hypothesises to explain these events. Test hypothesis' with reason and other events to narrow down number of explanations

We also create ideas from allegories other systems. Very different systems can have similar emergent effects if they have similar system structures. An example we use is the idea of distributed computing (Grid computers) and democracy/debate.

We can subject our ideas to critical debate, either by ourselves or with others. Criticism generates creativity.

In what follows we use these methods as guidelines for our thought, though we create a narrative that knits together these methods in a similar kind of reasoning to retroduction, that is to use the best method to tackle the problem, as opposed to separating reasoning into deductive and inductive knowledge.

The Universal Social model

This perhaps arrogant term is our description of our attempt to find a universal social model. We take Marx's concept of social forces and Jessop insight that social forces when blocked find other routes to achieve their aims, perhaps with more vigour. By social force, we mean many individuals who have an ideology, social norms, goals and who create an emergent effect (a characteristic of the group that emerges from the actions of all group members). So capitalism or the free market economy, has an ideology (economics), social norms (contract and company law), goals (profit) and creates an emergent effect (continual expansion over long periods of production and consumption in society). There is not necessarily agreement between agents of a social force, either tacit or written, (see the conflict between Iraqi Sunnis and shias) so this is very different from say a bureaucratic organisation such as the modern military. There is not necessarily a central leader though some parts of the social force are more influential than others and the archetypes of the ideas that motivate and generate the social force's world view may be from old ideas, such as the possibility that Sayid Qutb's writings give the Islamic radicals of today much of their ideology.

We suggest that social forces have both a potential and realised energy. The potential energy is the pent up desires of the groups that form the social force to carry out actions in respect of their ideology and goals. Realised energy is the riot, the speech, the applause, the overthrow. Potential energy may either fall or increase in response to realised energy occurring. A group may become worn out, or it may be spurred on to greater heights.

We look at recent theories of society, memetics, particularly the mathematical models of nodes in networks, with a node each representing a person in society and the links between the nodes representing communication between each node which all form a large and complex network. While we dismiss the models given by this literature, the basic framework is kept, that is of nodes passing messages to other nodes. We expand on this. A node will have a filter, similar to the idea of an activation function in neural networks, that blocks, enhances or changes messages that come to the node.

From Gramsci, we take the idea that there are interests in society. The interests, or desires, of an individual will affect the messages that they accept. Ideas will often be rejected if they are against a person's interests and will often become warped to fit their desires and prejudices. What interests are there in AA? It is not correct that a non-racist person will find AA in their interests, except as they may perceive that it is sending a message to the US to stop or carry out a policy or value. Identity will define a persons interests as will economic status and historical factors.

The progress of an idea, its metamorphosis as it travels across society inter and intra-generationally, is determined by the methodology of the group that discuss the idea. From Popper, an Open System ,or one that allows criticism will create better ideas by cutting away at bad parts of ideas until we reach the ideal truth. From Hegel, we suggest that ideas are created through criticism which eventually reaches the ideal. We argue below that democracy is a valid system for quickly reaching the ideal.

We can look at ideas in the relations they have with each other, for example anthropology and sociology are linked as social science, though they contain different methodologies and have contradictory concepts, heterogeneity in the former and homogeneity in the latter at different levels to each other. Ideas form massive idea maps and are part of social forces' ideologies.

There is information compression as ideas spread across the network, which leads ,from Shannon, to signal degradation, that is the information content of the message deteriorates as it goes through the network.

Some ideas are archetypes, that is there is a fuzzy logic relation between ideas throughout history and across different parts of the world and society. Marxism comes from the Christianity archetype since they are based on similar privilege of the poor, though this is a fuzzy identity. We can identify similarities which can lead us to arguing that different ideas are linked through time by comparing similarities in their idea maps.

Social norms are rules and values that are part of a social force. They generate can generate energy when they are violated by another group, and also they generate action and evolution of strategies. A social norm to dress differently to others will lead to a continually changing set of styles of fashion, though the desire for conformity will lead to archetypes being held to, as will the technical competence of producers of clothes.

The limitation of bureaucracy may lead to social forces using a distributed organisation and decision making structure. This is the division of the command structure into many sources, with the piecemeal approach to solving problems across many participants.

The Universal Social Model Applied to Democracy

Free speech, free values (that is the toleration of alternative value systems), free universities and also a free press leads to a greater amount of creation, adaptation and synthesis of ideas through debate.

Open debate that is progressive requires criticism, which leads to new ideas being created to overcome opposition, and also listening, that is people must be prepared to learn from others, so all ideas are transmitted across the network and allowed to synthesise. This leads to maximum creation of new ideas and thus greater choice. Whether or not people should have a filter is difficult to analyse since the filter changes ideas to fit interests in society. An ideal debating team or parliament as we call it, will require many individuals, some who are against each other and some who are more objective and do not have much of a filter outside of the rational. Indeed a few wise madmen with no filter whatsoever may even be useful.

Democracy is argued to be progressive as we have outlined it. Clearly there can be many forms of democracy which all produce the same effect. The main thing needed is a group of heterogeneous people who are creative, representative of all interests and understand or can learn a large range of issues.

Democracy has the ability to distribute decision making and problem solving to create novel and representative solutions which are in line with the interests of society. The ability to overcome paradigm limitations due to free values, makes the need for democracy in society ever more pressing, and the need for people to understand how democracy really works to create solutions that authoritarian, despotic regimes are less well able to create.

While the UK parliament has both an objective unfiltered aspect, the House of Lords, and a more filtered interest representing group, the House of Commons, the problem with this system is that they do not continually debate critically between each other in one house. The problem is the limitations of either house would possibly be transmitted mimetically across the group making the house either very objective or very interest particularly short term political interest orientated.

The problem with knowledge is that it is often influenced politically. This may lead to a hegemony occurring with an elite's interest controlling knowledge. This applies to parliament as well. The way to avoid this problem is to have knowledge representing a wide variety of interests and for those interests to be allowed free rein in debate. The limitation of participants in debate as well as the restriction of different subjects methodology prevent knowledge from being applied well to existing problems. The slow change in knowledge to keep up with present issues is also a problem. The limitation of subject matter allows elites to take control as well. These criticisms also apply to parliament as well.

Traditional democracy is representative. The voters choose someone who is essentially an accountable limited term dictator. We suggest a new route to solving the problems of the world and society.

In short we suggest having everyone enter into debates which they choose to enter giving ideas on how to solve problems in the interests of society. This would create a better democracy. The theoretical basis of this is distributed computing. Essentially this is where many people each contribute to the solution of a problem. The fact of the matter is that people each have a limited amount of mental capacity, so if a problem is broken down and given to many people who each solve part of the problem, much more complex problems can be solved. This is also similar to the production technique known as Open Source used in the creation of Linux. Clearly this requires an educated society and more resources should be ploughed into initial and ongoing education, rational thought and critical thinking.

The essence of this new democracy is to be found in debate. The many participants would contribute their ideas to a forum, perhaps on the internet, and would debate the relative merits of their ideas. Criticism is essential for this process to work, maintaining quality of debate and ideas. People would be stimulated by seeing the forum and create even more ideas and solutions. The lack of need for voting on ideas would be counterbalanced by the fact that anyone could enter the debate and criticise any idea. The debate would need people to realise that they must be constructive and respectful to others. The debate would also have its guiding principal of finding consensus among participants. We should stress that these debates are not a substitute for existing democratic institutions like parliament, but essentially they would create another house in parliament, one in cyberspace. The House of Everyone. While this house would have no legal powers it would impact on the debate in the other houses of parliament, simply because it would generate better ideas that would be in line with people's feelings on various matters. A team of moderators would go through the forum and find common themes in the debates and write articles summarising the common points people make. These articles would be available on the forum and would stimulate the generation of yet more ideas. Articles would also be available on the constraints facing governments written by civil servants and academics which would give people a better idea of how to tackle problems which society faces. Instead of the debate in society being divided into various interest groups lobbying parliament, people would interact in one forum to create a united Britain.

Legitimacy is created in this kind of democracy through everyone feeling like they have contributed to policy. This would solve the government's main problem which is to legitimise itself. This is in opposition to the Neo-Conservative idea of the "noble lie" where governments don't tell the masses everything to enable them to believe in the government.

More ideas would be created and also ideas would be generated that were in line with existing thinking of the people of society. Why should one only have a say when the election comes?

What is anti-Americanism?

Anti-Americanism is a term used to describe the many different processes and reactions to America as a nation-state in existence and in action. It relates to world views, ideas, discourses and narratives associated with many different groups in many different countries.

As a phenomena that is fundamentally a mental act of information compression to describe reactions to Cultural Hegemony such as the predominance of Hollywood, to American values (different parts of the spectrum of values in the US are seen by varying groups as bad), to the progress of US policy in various parts of the world.

As a master narrative, an era defining global story, it takes on the character of universal truth across cultures. It defines an external other, a threat to all. In this sense the very idea of AA is actually a danger to America, especially if people are not afraid to be AA. However, the category implies racism on the part of the anti-american, and so is likely to coerce people to react against it.

We will not take on the division of legitimate criticism of the US and illegitimate criticism. Such subjective categories cannot be universally identified. To take on such categories would be to interact in the debate on the US.

The take we have on Anti-Americanism is to look at the mechanisms and processes that underlie it. The use of a blanket term is useful only insofar as we look at the processes that it is caused by and causes. The subdivision of the term into the Anti-American left, AA Muslims, etc, is also useful because it is likely that these social groups will have an internal dynamic, though we must also look at the interaction between the groups. For example, demonstrations by the Stop the War Coalition involved British Muslim groups as well, an alliance of the left, peace activists and Islam in the UK.

Thus we look at all kinds of processes, attitudes, policies and ideologies as well as narratives and discourses that are against the interest or the being of the United States of America. We define this as AA.

The fundamental problem with this definition is that AA does not take into account the fact that a policy of the US is formulated in conjunction with other pressures including the opinion of others outside of the US. If a policy is bad for the world then the US may well consider the value of AA. Thus AA is not necessarily a bad thing, indeed as we mention in our theory of democracy, exchange of ideas from different viewpoints creates progress.

AA is not just a set of ideas, it is a kind of mindset that alters the perception of the viewer of international events to colour them in a different anti-american light. Conspiracy theories about the CIA being involved in operations without evidence are examples of the AA mindset. In this sense is best seen as an idea map whereby historical narratives with America as an idea and political entity being linked to promotion of immoral or illegal activity, such as war, assassination, coup d'etats, torture, discrimination and double standards, inaction in respect of genocide, promotion of instability in countries, trade sanctions and disputes, anti-environmental activity, lying and trickery. It is interesting to look at the similarity of Anti-Americanism as an idea map and the development of the Western idea map of Islam.

There is also the question of which America are we talking about. If we look at the split in recent elections in the US between Democrat and Republican lines, there is a liberal element and a reactionary conservative element. Some anti-Americans are not in opposition of the more liberal more dovish sentiments of the political establishment which begs the question whether anti-Americanism is really a reaction to the right by the left.

The problem is really that America does not take into account the political viewpoints of others outside of its system, which leads to problems. If the AA social groups are to become effective they must try to engage in dialogue with Americans to convince them of better ways of solving common problems rather than creating hatred of America. This is the deep rooted and myopic nature of AA. It is a social phenomena, an emergent effect of many different social groups and processes, that acts as a beast on its own rather than an amalgamation of many different conscious beings with free will and reason. Related to the emergent (unwilled and macro-systemic) nature of AA is the current Western idea of Islam as an evil to be confronted, tortured, converted and if that does not occur, destroyed. When one looks at ones enemy what one often sees is oneself. Later we will discuss the Western viewpoint of Islam as 'Islamofascism'. What we argue there relates to the point that idea maps once set in history and consensually accepted can take on a dynamic of their own in informing and structuring relations later on, perhaps expressed in violence and religious/ethnic deportation.

The interesting development is the substitution of anti-Americanism in the world's idea map with Islam as a problem, whether through so called terrorism or supposed oppressive practices by sovereign Islamic nation-states. Clearly Anti-Americanism, which came to a height in the late 20th Century brought a reaction from US policy elites to substitute the critical faculty of its society towards Muslims. Clearly this also has the effect of legitimising domination of one of the world's richest supplies of oil while also providing an external threat to create a feeling of a united social group in the US and among its allies and thus reduce contestation. It has to be seen as a grand and powerful plan by US elites. The fact that Muslims have made a robust response to this plan shows the lack of forward thinking which is endemic in the US.

The Left

We shall discuss the Left wing peace movement of the UK during the 21st Century in its contestation of the Official government narrative and policy. The official government narrative was that history begins on September 11th 2001 (often termed 9/11), when the world trade centre in America was destroyed by terrorists who were Muslims. To understand why the left contested the official story of the government we discuss several related ideas that were causing a shift in understanding of the world as it was then. The left was visible in peace demonstrations in London, with socialist worker party banners peppered through the march and members of the Labour party present, such as Tony Benn.

The Left's social norms are generated by the historical development of this social group as well as the archetypes of what is seen as good for the ordinary working class person. This means that institutions like the trade unions, implements or strategies for obtaining good for the working class are a social norm, privileged even though many in the left have the common British dislike of power concentrated.

Vietnam was a period when the Left were against the conduct of American foreign policy. This created an archetype, that is a common thread in ideas and stories across time and space, that has come again in the interpretation of events after the 9/11 attacks. The impact of defeat in Vietnam on the cultural psyche of the West lead many to draw parallels between Vietnam and the invasions of Muslim countries that followed 9/11. Essential to this idea is that expectations of defeat of the US were high, but also the real cost of war was thoroughly and graphically understood by peace movement members. The tension between the Left and the US government's foreign policy is found historically, since Lenin spoke of the US's "Imperialist capitalist" policies. This too has formed an archetype that has come together with the Vietnam interpretation and created a strong backlash against the war by the Left. After the difficulties of the Iraq invasion there was a considerable diffusion of the Left's arguments as theory became dreadful reality.

The left has had an old narrative that the source of progress by capitalism is violence and theft. This forms an archetypal idea that moves through the generations and finds its new version in the form of reducing America's motivation for invasion of the Middle East to the desire for oil. Clearly if oil were the major objective then the administration wouldn't have embarked on the invasions of Muslim countries since we have seen the oil price rise to very high levels in recent years. This assumes basic economic knowledge guiding the US government. There are plausibly several considerations for the true motivation of US foreign policy. Firstly there is the winds and currents of prevailing thought (such as neo-conservatism), the history of the US facing sustained criticism from all quarters whether from others or its own people lead to a reaction to ignore and deflect dissent and contestation, replacing this with a forceful, myopic drive for American interests, as seen by the US administration. The issue of an external threat giving rise to less contestation within the nation-state, through distraction along with reproduction and reinforcement of the institutions of the nation-state is clearly a good though complex explanation for US behaviour. The America of the late 20th century was a place where groups were engaged in challenging the idea of that age 'Globalisation'. The collapse of the internet bubble that lead to a recession in the US came just before 9/11. These conditions explain some of the overbearing reaction of the US government to 9/11. However we must make clear that explanation and moral justification are two different subjects, social theory/historical analysis and moral philosophy.

The left has been pacified by the argument, from Hayek, that socialism is good but requires terrible violence to achieve itself, the example of Stalin being the key point. This narrative, which has shades of Christianity, is part of the process that leads many in the left to call for peace.

The left's social norm of disarmament and lack of militarism in the UK labour party is possibly something that has been nurtured by the establishment to pacify it. This too has been a key source of the acceptance of the 'peace' message.

The effect of the 9/11 "Thou shalt not kill" message created by this event is to have generated a great deal of impetus for a peace movement. The left do not have a category of them and us, i.e. they see people from other countries as equals. This means that they strive to have rules that are universal, in the sense that they are founded on the Liberal equality archetype. They take it as self-evident that all are born equal. The left therefore has a key driver of anti-racism and promote the involvement and peaceful, respectful engagement with different ethnic groups.

Some of the rational criticism of US foreign policy in respect of Muslims is based around a model of terrorism, implicitly held by adherents to the Left's peace movement. The rallying call of the Left Peace movement is that the US administration is the biggest recruiter of terrorists who attack the West. What the model is composed of is that the history of double standards in US foreign policy is directly linked to the motivation for Muslims to become terrorists. In this way it is implied that the US administrations of the late 20th and early 21st century are implicated in creating terrorism through providing provocation of Muslims. We will discuss Bin Laden's input into the Islamic praxitioner jihad's idea map later, where we will see that this model is founded on a thorough analysis of his argument for jihad. What is argued by the left is that there is a deviation of the goal of the West, as understood by the Left to be peaceful relations with Muslims, from policy, which in the early 21st Century involves heavy handed attacks and military invasion by American forces. The model that the left has of terrorism is that it is motivated by a desire to stop American attacks, occupation and murder of Muslims. Therefore the US policy of invasion to stop terror is thrown into a contradiction. If the cause of terror is the reaction to Muslims being killed and their lands being occupied then a policy of invasion of Muslim countries becomes self-defeating. Thus the left argues that there is a deviation of goals from policy.

Below is summarized the key points we have discussed above to produce what is an idea map for the left's peace movement from the UK after 9/11/2001. This idea map must be seen in a relation of tension to the existing narrative of the US government as to the best response to the issue of a worldwide Islamic jihad being fought.

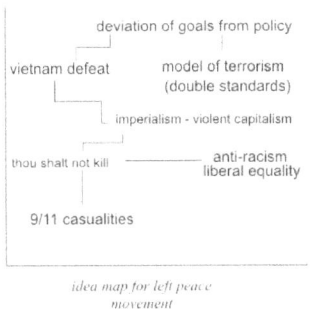

idea map for left peace movement

Islam

Much of the hatred of America by Muslims is likely to be a recent thing, for example Islam predates America so it is not possible for Islam to be inherently anti-American.

Islam has social norms or rules in respect of Jihad, which state that "Fight those who fight you". They also have rules saying that if an enemy wants peace, you should also accept peace. The former rule generates an idea map which links American foreign policy with these rules of the Quran. The extent of the penetration of this idea map is hard to determine, it would change from day to day with events. But we can tell that much of Islamic anger is generated by this idea map and it is the source of Islamic AA. As we can see idea maps create effects in the minds of the holders of them, especially when one sees the idea map of US foreign policy history with intervention in Iraq and lack of any action on genocide in Bosnia. The reasoning basis is one of the US constitution that all people are born free and equal though this has its origins in reasoning from religious books where all people are the same before God.

The history of Islamic anti-Americanism is primarily, unlike early European AA, due to US foreign policy. Since the 1953 American sponsored coup in Iran that imposed the West leaning monarchy, there has been substantial dislike of America.

We hypothesise that it was a simple AA of objection to policy, which created potential energy in the Islamic social forces, and thus lead to the creation of hatred for America and the new realised energy of terrorism. Terrorism did not start with many of the US's recent wars, but it was possibly motivated by US involvement in the Middle East region. The fact that the nascent Al Quaeda was prepared and even welcomed US help in overcoming the Russians in Afghanistan suggests that at this time anti-Americanism was not prevalent.

Islam does not value criticism as much as other groups particularly of scholars of Islam. Thus the part that ideas play in the Islamic social force are simply archetypes, ideas from earlier ideas, which is essentially the main reasoning process that occurs in Islamic jurisprudence as formalized by Shafi'i. Therefore ideas in Islam will tend not to evolve as much as ideas in other groups like the Left. On the other hand, there will be greater tendencies of consensus in this social force because there are fewer ideas accepted.

A current in thinking concerning the Jihad movement of the modern world is that the seed of it was spread from Sayyid Qutb's argument of the process of Islam; politically and socially. It has sometimes been cited that Qutb formed the archetype that lead to Bin Laden. It is possible that the message of Qutb has propagated across the network of Muslims or it is possible that actions of America created the credibility of Qutb's message. Racism is a possible reason for Qutb's message propagating though it is possible that Qutb is not the main reason for AA racism propagating. Many people affected by US foreign policy may have the same thoughts concurrently without any propagation. These thoughts then give Qutb, Bin Laden and others messages more credibility.

We discuss the idea map of the modern Jihad movement from a textual analysis of Bin Laden's messages. The western media typically reports excerpts from them, which is very telling, considering the fact that if one has nothing to hide then one listens to the opponents arguments and engages with them. The fact that the whole narrative of the war on terror and international Jihad has become a series of overlapping stories in the sense of being near impossible to complete discuss without being contradictory means that we must focus on core mechanisms that drive the whole system of relations between Muslims and the West. Above all we are interested in sociological explanation rather than moral questions of who is right or wrong. Taking this as an approach we hope to elucidate more of the picture rather than paint over reality with our prejudices.

Bin Laden has given many messages to the world. It is difficult to separate the political Bin Laden, that is the one who wishes to move people in certain directions, and the real one, that is the one who represents his personal feelings on matters. Clearly though his messages are above this dichotomy since they affect people as they are interpreted by them. They are fairly unambiguous messages so we do not have to consider the possible variation in interpretation. Unequivocally he calls for global jihad against what he sees as a Judeao-Crusader Alliance, which one assumes is America and Israel with possibly Britain involved too and this may refer to Europe as well. He sees it as a defensive jihad to deter the killing of Muslims, particularly civilians.

He creates a narrative that suggests that the modern history of the Muslim people is one of being a victim of aggression by non-Muslims. He singles out America for most of the blame. He connects this historical narrative to previous ones, suggesting that the fall of Andalucía (southern Spain which was controlled by the moors) could happen to Muslim lands particularly Saudia Arabia. His reservations and anger over US foreign policy, both its actions and inactions, are shared by a great many Muslims. This is a reaction to information from the media about Muslim deaths and torture which stimulates natural human reactions as part of group behaviour as well as reactions from rules given in the Quran regarding the viewing of all Muslims as one group and also viewing the justification of killing in response to killing as a valid course of action. What Bin Laden does though is to override rules that civilians are not allowed to be killed in battle. He also mirrors Bush's initial reaction to 9/11 of 'you're either with us or against us', with a declaration that any Muslim who helps America in its invasion is defined as a target of the Jihad movement and is considered an apostate.

Since Bin Laden was not carrying out terrorism since his early youth, it would seem plausible that the actions of the US came to bring about his ideas linking Islamic theology to military strategy under the motivation of historical relations. Curiously enough he does not go back to the British imperial mistakes with regard to the Muslim world perhaps due to the decline of the empire. Were Bin Laden to be concertedly against non-Muslims then he could certainly draw on the colonial legacy of Britain. But Britain no longer influences the world. Therefore his Jihad is limited to the material well being of Muslims rather than something that one can say is caused by a hatred of non-Muslims.

An interesting digression is the reaction of Bin Laden to the peace movement in the West. He describes peace activists as "polite and good people". What becomes clear from this comment is that he does not intrinsically hate the West's people. Discussion with many Muslims show a similar attitude. We see here a great concordance between the Left wing model of terrorism and Bin Laden's idea map, that it is motivated on achieving peaceful relations between Muslims and the West, in other words terror is a strategic response to Western foreign policy that murders Muslims rather than an existential discordance. The response of the Left to 9/11, by creating a peace movement, leaves Muslims with a Foucaudian problem in determining the correct theological rule to follow in terms of the exercise of Jihad. This is stated as whether the agency in question is the state (which wants war) or the people (who want peace, as given by the existence of a peace movement).

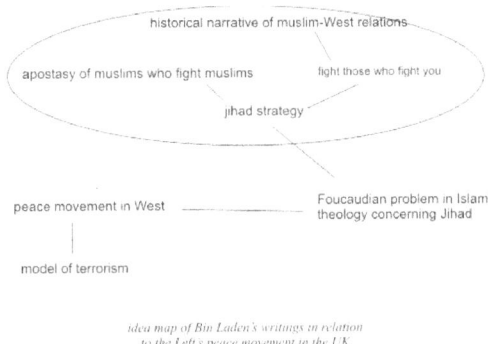

idea map of Bin Laden's writings in relation to the Left's peace movement in the UK

Islamo-fascism; an example of idea map analysis in the policy of justifying mass murder of Muslims

Another area of interest is the term "Islamofascism". This is the linking of two ideas, Islam and fascism. Islam was created in the 7th century and was not linked to Fascism which was essentially created by Hitler in the 20th Century. Islam did not develop into Fascism. Hitler was not a Muslim. A key idea in Fascism is the asserted superiority of the Aryan race. Muslims are of all ethnic groups and there is no ordering according to ethnicity. The only similarity is that Muslims and Nazis are both people who America has been at war with. Muslims are fighting against the mass murder of their people by Americans, that is simply the text of their argument to encourage Muslims to fight America. Nazi's wanted to colonise the colonisers of Europe. In no area of Bin Laden's texts does he state that he wishes to overthrow the American government or establish the superiority of the Aryan ethnic group. The lack of reason in idea maps is perhaps no where more evident that here. The fact that ideas are linked together often in short phrases that have a resonance and popularity without rationale could begin our search to understand culture more and lead us to insight into this deeply symbiotic part of the human and society.

The popularity of the term Islamofascism and ascription on people as being Islamo-fascists is the most banal and obvious pomp to justify American mass murder of Muslims, whether past, present or future. It is interesting to note that such an idea can exist even though reason would suggest that it was incompatible with the historic meaning of the very terms it compresses together. Its potency is largely because it encapsulates a spirit of the age of the de facto racially segregated-fascist America. Its effect is to halt the democratic contestation process of US policy against Muslims, past and present. Its implication is that Fascist are evil, therefore they must die, Muslims are Fascists, therefore they must die. The idea map for Islamofascism must be seen as interlinked with this syllogism. What is interesting is determining which body created this term, since it colludes well with the assumptions and goals of 21st Century American foreign policy.

The result of linking Islam with Fascism without much in the way of reasoned argument allows an instant discrediting of Islam and impetus without justification for murder of Muslims. There is the paradox that hatred of Muslims caused by the terms 'Islamofascism' could follow a path along the same lines as the growth of Anti-Semitism in early 20th Century Europe, which culminated in the mass murder of Jewish people.

21. On Shafi'i- an early formaliser of Islamic theological methodology/Jurisprudence

While Islam is understood by its adherents to be a complete system, there is distinct difference among various thinkers in a number of aspects of its specific rules. For example Sayyid Qutb produces an Islamic argument for jihad as a process and strategy for the creation of a nation-state of Islam by connecting various verses in the Quran out of order. On the other hand we would privilege the rule deriving from the verses "if you kill someone then it is as if you have killed all of humanity". As you can see very different actions can be suggested to be good depending on where we start in our premises, even if we are in a debate where all parties accept the same central texts for derivation of rules. This argument ties in with a core theme of this book which is that debate will lead along many different avenues and with different results even when a common rational process is used for production of argument. This digression tells us the limitation of belief that ones rational arguments can be held without criticism, whether in economics or Islamic theology.

At the core of Shariah is the determination of the objective of it, in other words a metanarrative on the meaning of life and existence in the next one. Shafi'I, we argue makes Shariah a tool for reproduction of the Islamic Ummah (social group). He is weaker on the alternative objectives for Shariah, one of which is to maximise the number of people who go to heaven. The second point we make is that while there are a vast swathe of rules emanating from the religious texts, there is less developed argument and justification as to the methodology of the interpretation and application of the rules from religious texts. Shafi'I was a noted scholar in Islamic theology who brought together the main currents in thinking up to that time and developed a systematic method for the production of rules from the Quran and Sunnah. We seek to see if his method stands up to enquiry. It would be of great consequence to Muslims if there were more to be said as to how one makes a rule and who makes the rules. At the heart of our argument is the intention to maximise the amount of goodness in the world and we see that an important channel for this to occur is through the coherence of Islamic rules and goodness. We follow Shafi'I in producing our argument in concordance with Islam by isolating the key, perhaps overlooked issue in understanding what it means to be good.

Shafi'i restricts the production of rules of Islam to a small elite of Arabic speaking scholars. He rails against juristic preference (istihsan) through providing a systematic methodology for production of rules (direct rules and qiyas generated rules). This can be seen as a interesting sociological device for maintaining the consistency and integrity of the Ummah. Alternatively one can see that Shafi'I is responding to the Quran and Sunnah, or at least parts of them, to create these rules, notably when he says in the Risala that Muslims must not divide into sects.

It is possible that the reason that Shafi'I chose to restrict and systematise the production of religious rules is to reduce cultural drift (i.e. small changes in different geographical areas) leading to splits in Islam. At the end of the day, Shariah has one obvious objective, to maximise the number of people who go to heaven. A judgement of Shafi'I rests on assessment of whether his influential organisation of Islamic religious authority, which has an impact on political and social institutions, actually can be argued to lead to the most people going to heaven. Since mankind is imperfect and scholars are a subset of mankind then they may make mistakes, especially when their rules are followed under different conditions and periods of history. It is too great a burden to place on scholars to find perfect timeless rules from Islamic texts, given that different situations, different times in history, call for different assessment of the good, thus a scholar would need to be all knowing in order to produce a perfect interpretation. In addition everyone is responsible for their own actions, thus one cannot call to a scholar to intercede for us and save us from Hell should we find ourselves to be judged as engaging in wrong doing by following an erroneous rule written by a scholar.

We also could contest whether the most acceptable goal of Shariah is the maximisation of people going to heaven. In the Salat (prayer) of Islam, at the end a Muslim recites "Our Lord! Give us the Good in this world and the Good in the next one." Thus one could reasonably argue that a Muslim should be considerate of obtaining good in the material world (being moderate), whilst also trying to obtain good in terms of getting into heaven (in other words being an extremist or fundamentalist). Thus we argue that Muslims should be neither extremists nor moderates but rather moderate-extremists.

The weakness in Shafi'I's argument is that the implied premise on which his restriction of juristic preference and ijhtihad is based upon is that there are no good deeds possible that are not specified in the Quran and Sunnah as understood directly or by analogy. Otherwise he would have promoted other means to finding out ideas that are doing good in addition to qiyas and direct interpretation of the source texts.

We can give an example of how there are other ideas that are good which are not specified in the Quran and Sunnah. For example, it is good to be kind to one's parents. But whether this involves buying flowers for them or buying a watch for them depends on the character and needs of one's parents. It is clear that one needs a synthetic moral argument, that of bringing together principals and values to knowledge of the circumstance. The question we pose is how far can one apply this to a general case of judging morally good action?

In summary Shafi'I is strong on producing a technique for managing the development of Muslims as a unified force yet is weaker on the actual meaning of good action, thought and being. We suggest an alternative metanarrative, which is that goodness is striving for a balance between the effects of action on this world and the effects on the next (heaven or hell).

22. Causes of poverty, a short literature review

Abstract

We summarise the main developments in the approach to understand and tackle poverty. We expose the main weakness in this literature which is the absence of a macro model of income and assets. We outline the idea of a macro framework based on concepts from the dynamic systems literature. We discuss other failings in the research as well as the solution to poverty through trade.

Poverty causes in the literature

Mainstream economists see the problem of poverty as one of asset endowment and stochastic shocks (ill health, famine) as well as conditions in economies (local, national and international) (Baulch and Hoddinott, 2000).
Political economy sees the external environment as often shaped by systematic factors, particularly unequal power relations. (Wood and Salway, 2000).
Sociologists and anthropologists look at household structures and relations (Francis, 2000). In addition, people's ability to gain access to assets, and their ability to translate them into income, are shaped by the workings of labour and product markets, by their access to skills, information and social networks, by norms governing resource use within and beyond the household and by gendered power relations, again within and beyond households.

Livelihood approaches broadened the object of enquiry from income and assets to capabilities, assets and activities required for living. Prospective livelihood approaches, typically adopted by development practitioners, attempt to identify potential means for improving livelihoods through interventions and better co-ordination of sectorally-based agencies.

Francis (2006) argues that in Madigobo, a large South African village, has many people who are on the edge of poverty principally because they do not have regular incomes and they actively migrate looking for increasingly casualised work. Seeking security of income is the tendency of their behaviour. Clearly regular incomes need to be created to fit in with the desires of the poor.

Left wing institutional analysis suggests that poverty is systemic, in other words there are sinks in the economic system which draw money towards them from the poor, for example the landlord in rural India that uses political, economic, social and legal power to maintain their superiority over the poor farmer tenants of their land. Using this as an archetype we can see that even in developed countries with welfare states there is the presence of a systemic poverty with paths leading towards crime, drugs, alcohol dependency and exclusion from society. Conversation tree analysis in poor areas and classes can be a potential area of cultural analysis whereby one can see from experience that there is a tendency to lower expectations of what one is capable of doing and thus social mobility is blunted, whilst social problems are enhanced. Just as the change in language against sexist comments, jokes, in other words changing the idea maps related to gender, helped to reduce the alienation of women in contemporary Western society, so too an understanding of what generates the self-identity idea map of people who are poor generation after generation, alongside the institutional and social systemic context, may all together lead to new solutions to poverty in rich countries and drastic reductions in crime.

Sinks in a dynamic system of income

The flow of money is seen to be the main focus of enquiry. This can be seen at a national level as a dynamic system that has sinks or attractors. These centres of gravity attract money into them, though they often recycle this money outward. An example of an attractor is the state. Many people give tax revenue to the state. Politically powerful individuals and organisations receive money from the state particularly in a clientist state. Chain stores are other examples of sinks which receive money from large numbers of consumers and then send it on to banks. The banking sector is a crucial sink since it recycles the cash held by it in the form of often productive loans for investment, boosting asset prices and also productivity. The problem in many developing countries that leads to poverty is that there are sinks which draw money away from the poor and do not recycle this. So traders will take money from the poor in exchange for goods but not invest this money in new jobs. Fundamentally there is the problem of the amount of value in the economy. This is the amount of income generated by organisations and individuals which is constrained by the finite demand for goods and is also a result of the bargaining process and capabilities of these people as well as the initial endowment of assets. Low levels of investment have classically been seen as the source of the low income of LDCs. This would be the capabilities limitation. But the absence of a high value bargaining process, as for example the relationship of marketing in developed countries, means that markets are underdeveloped. Many things that could potentially be produced are not in developing countries because of the low incomes of individuals and therefore the small market size that is present there.

The problem with the existing analysis of poverty in the literature

The point that is missed by all poverty literature is that money is limited in developing countries. The initial endowment is low, the amount of value able to be produced by the capabilities of the country is low and the amount of value that can be generated by selling goods within the economy, that is the level of demand, is low. There is a frugal approach to poverty in order to privilege the most desperate of cases of poverty, thus missing the fact that the country needs to become rich to solve these problems.

Gore (2003) suggests that trade is the source of the elimination of poverty. But there is an absence of the nexus of organisations and capacity building as well as the development of the value increasing process for products produced in the LDC.

A left wing criticism of the trade solution to poverty is that it focuses on the development of high value adding business which creates a middle class and excludes the poor. While there may be some social mobility, there are always a limited number of high value adding jobs. Globalisation that focuses primarily on developing small numbers of elite jobs thus chips away at poverty, since more income is being generated in the economy, but does not tackle the big question of how to raise the incomes and wealth of the poor majority.

Bibliography

Baulch, B. and J. Hoddinott (2000) 'Economic Mobility and Poverty Dynamics in Developing Countries', Introduction to a Special Issue of the Journal of Development Studies, 36(6): 1-24.

Francis, E. (2000) Making a Living: Changing Livelihoods in Rural Africa, London: Routledge.

Francis, E (2006) Poverty: Causes, Responses and Consequences in Rural South Africa , CPRC working paper, http://www.chronicpoverty.org/resources/working_papers.html

Gore, C. (2003). Globalization, the International Poverty Trap and Chronic Poverty in the Least Developed Countries. Working Paper 30. Manchester: IDPM/Chronic Poverty Research Centre (CPRC).

Wood, G. and S. Salway (2000) 'Introduction: Securing Livelihoods in Dhaka Slums', Journal of International Development 12(5): 669-688.

23. The nature of terrorism

Terrorism carried out by Muslims in the modern world does not have a clear organised structure. It is very far from a bureaucracy in form yet it is in a sense a rule based organisation, it is a rule based social force. There is no commander in chief, yet there are prominent members such as Osama Bin Laden, whose statements trigger action. Whether Osama Bin Laden is a product of the social force of Islam or the instigator is a difficult philosophical question that depends on one's view of agency in social structure.

The Muslim terrorist possibly takes much of his motivation from interpretations of the Quran and Sunnah, through the words of Scholars or directly from their own reading. Muslims are rule based individuals. Clearly this is not a satisfactory explanation since the arguments of jihadists often take verses of the Quran out of context or without the balancing injunctions in other parts of the Quran. As the mufti of Saudia Arabia has said Sheikh Abdul Aziz, the terrorist attacks of 9/11 were an act of oppression which is forbidden in Islam. So there is debate within the Muslim social force, with Osama Bin Laden talking of "fighting those who fight you" while others perhaps accept this but choose different peaceful tactics, the jihad of the heart (opposing the oppression of Muslims in one's mind). Who will win this debate? And what factors determine which way the debate goes?

But we digress, the motivations of the human mind to action can be modelled as a neural network in AI. This suggests that a multitude of factors will add up and push a decision to act once the total value is over a tipping point, an activation function is pushed into firing a signal to other neurons. Clearly the level of the activation function and the connections between different neurons (factors) varies with each individuals experiences. This analysis suggests that we should be looking for many variables which motivate terrorism.

We can augment the rule based model of Muslims to include a variety of interpretations of Islam that depend on events and messages that they see and receive respectively. The interpretations are caused by events and messages. This would account possible for the hardening in stance of Bin Laden as seen by his messages both before and after the Afghan invasion by the US and also for his interesting reaction to seeing a peace movement develop in places like the UK, an event / message that made him partition the West into "good, honest people" and others.

The structure of terrorist groups in the Muslim world is sometimes confused with Al-Quaeda, the Mujahadeen from the Afghan war with the Soviets. While current terrorists are likely to be influenced by Al-Quaeda it is likely given the global scale of terrorism and the lack of ability of leaders such as Osama Bin Laden to communicate because of the risk of being captured, that they only share an ideology, a set of ideas that determine their actions and goals. There is also the dynamic recruitment process, whereby actions that lead to the death and suffering of Muslims serve to create more recruits for terrorists. The climate of fear among Muslims leads to some to find a stable world that protects them by their subjective transactions with God, protection from harm in exchange for adherence to rules they believe were laid down by God. Thus these two factors both created by counter terrorism policy are problematic features of the current strategy to defeat terrorism. Since there is no strict command structure for all of the Muslim terrorist organisations and since they are very geographically dispersed this is unlikely to develop, the nature of terrorism is thus a social force. Similar to the nature of the free market economy, which is a cultural meme that spreads throughout the world, where some become entrepreneurs and others employees. They function on rules that determine their behaviour, in this case the profit making motive, through means within the law that supply the wants of people who are willing to pay for those wants. When blocked by regulation, say when there were usury laws, the social force finds a way through. The idea and motive is so strong that blocking its vital interests is sometimes difficult if not impossible. The powerful and widely dispersed nature of this phenomena means that society can outwit the social structure. Thus the free market economy wins over the state. The Islamic social force is possibly similar. The intensity of belief among Muslims is strongly developed and reproduced through institutions such as prayer, fasting and repetition of belief. The rules of Islam encourage Muslims to find pious people to be friends with. This leads to pockets of the faithful, possibly the fundamentalist, growing ever larger. The danger of a virulent and deadly meme legitimising murder to achieve the end of martyrdom, note not the solution to Muslims problems, is evident. Note that fear and repression as part of a counter terrorism policy are difficult to work advantageously since the outcome of the terrorists strategy is either fight and be martyred or fight and win.

24. The philosophical problem at the heart of dynamics of society

Do individual leaders make society or does society make the individual. Furthermore are processes involved viewable as individuals making grand ideas or are they reducible to psycho-social processes.

For example, the Islamic revival, alternatively specified as the rise of Islamic fundamentalism or the development of Islamic praxis can be seen as a series of books and ideas produced by thinkers. However this does not explain why ideas are spread and accepted by many people. They may for example have an interest in seeing ideas spread because the idea gives something of value to them. This is the Gramscian approach. Alternatively one can see the development of Islamic praxis as the search for coherency with Islamic values that is generated from the first Kalimah, there is no God but the One God and Muhammad is his messenger. This is taken from Velleman's insight that the mind seeks to create coherency to avoid, perhaps one could speculate in response to, an identity crisis. As a digression one wonders if the stimulation of Islamic praxis (the revival of Islam in the world) has been triggered or at least enhanced by Liberal postcolonial ideology of equality of all humans alongside oppressive double standards by America against Muslims. What we suggest is that the identity crisis for Muslims came when they saw themselves as equals yet were not treated as such and thus began to be receptive to ideas that compensated for this contradiction, which involved the coherence of their being, family, community, state and laws with Islamic teachings. Therefore rise of Islamic praxis (fundamentalism).

How do we determine which of the above 3 approaches is having the most effect on the outcome? Can we a priori determine this or is a historical inductive approach possible?

A historical approach would suggest that the search for consistency between Islamic life and Islamic teachings has resurfaced many times in Muslim history. Shafi'i's risala is an early 2nd century AH example of the limitation of Islamic teachings to a small elite who followed a consistent methodology in bringing together Islam with society in terms of law. Later movements like the followers of Ibn Taymiyaah which became the Wahabi ideology reproduced this approach with the emphasis on 'purifying Islam' from ideas that did not come from messengers of God. In the 20th Century Maudoudi built on the Marxist criticism of capitalism, Marx was his archetype. He influenced Qutb whose archetypal descendants include the Muslim brotherhood in Egypt and Al-Quaeda.

What this shows is that there are certainly some individuals more involved in creating ideas. But where do these ideas come from? Why is the overall thrust the same across many different cultures and times in history? One argument that would explain this is that the issue is psycho-social, that is the social process involved of establishing consistency between ideas and institutions originates from Velleman's search for consistency as a psychological process in the brain. The alternative hypothesis is the memetic model of information transmission across different social groups. The problem with this approach is that it does not shed any light on why ideas are consistently connected in their creation and acceptance. One could argue that this is simply a result of memetic transmission of ideas with signal degradation across nodes leading to similar ideas. However liberalism is another idea that has had strong dispersion but has not taken root with quite the same fervour as Islamic praxis. Indeed interaction with Islamic praxitioners leads one to believe that praxis leads to a sense of well-being for them. This is consistent with the Vellemanian consistency search.

Clearly there could be other processes, whether psycho-social or not, involved in the revival of Islam. However what we have is a simple model of the Ummah (the entire body of Muslims in the world) which gives an analytical insight into the direction of their evolution. It also explains why the current policy of combating so called extremism has been in all lights a failure.

25. Non-reductionist Memetic Theory in relation to Habermas and Dawkins

Dawkins's theory of ideas as an analogy with genes which he calls 'memes' are the building block of our analysis. He develops deductions of the characteristics of the most successful memes (ideas) in a similar way as biology predicts the characteristics of the most successful genes. The lack of empirical comparison and error-correction as well as the extreme reductionist flavour of Dawkin's memetic theory are his main flaws. Science that allows its analytical tools to engulf the clear, reasoned observation of the actual system in question, leads to errors as the process of change of the analytical tools deviates from the reality.

Our correction to Dawkin's memetic theory is to observe the system closer, that is the fact that while characteristics of ideas (memes) are important, the relations or links that these memes travel along are also vital to any successful model. These can be drawn out as a network composed of nodes, which broadly speaking link people to each other where they transfer ideas by way of conversation trees. Conversation trees are a compression of the sum total of heterogeneous debates that occur in society that either reinforce, establish newly or change peoples minds on a certain subject or belief, thereby leading to idea transference across the network. We suggest that conversations can reasonably be summarised into various categories, with key power words/arguments, drawing legitimacy from consensus idea maps present in society, used to produce consistent outcomes in debates. Just as many different employees can be categorised as the working class for analysis, we believe that the common threads and interactions involved in many debates can be summarised in each different area of thought and ideas. The reason why is because we assume that there is a finite set of rational ideas and of these a much smaller set of persuasive ideas.

Dawkins pursues the traditional scientific positivist goal of obtaining laws or generalities from axioms and principles through deduction. Memes that are shortest and easiest to understand by the largest section of the population will be the most likely to survive and also dominate. Our discussion is that the result is very sensitive to network configuration. For example the largest section of the population may be poorly linked together. Whereas certain richer sections of the population may be linked to the entire network via the media or interest groups. Also a smaller group may be more densely linked (analogous and indeed a major causal point in the Olsonian big/small argument). Another point is that people may summarise ideas leading to information compression in order to facilitate their wider and faster flow through the network. This leads to signal degradation or information loss that means that the best ideas must be those that can easily be summarised even if they are long to begin with. This underlies our belief that the predictions of memetics can never be very clear since evaluating how and how well a person will summarise an idea is impossible to analyse since people are of different intellectual ability and indeed may find it easy to summarise one idea but not another.

Another pertinent difficulty with Dawkin's thesis is that the flow of ideas extends not just across agents but along generations, thus the concept of tradition is built.
Habermas' theory of lifeworlds, formed from the traditional culture, network and process of socialisation, as apart from system (state and capital) is distinguished from our theory by the focus we have on ideas moving around networks of people and institutions. Habermas did not consider communicative action to be something individuals created but rather something they received from their lifeworld. Our model suggests that people may hold many ideas essentially have many life-worlds but whether they choose one or another depends on their interests and also the state of the system, i.e. if there is a consensus then they will hold that idea.

That said there is some validity to the approach to synthesise our ideas with Habermas since they deal with a similar subject matter. Specifically his ideas of credibility of a speech act, in our model 'a message', as being governed by 1) how near a message is to the state of affairs in the world 2) how near it follows a set of norms 3) how credible is the speaker, would tell us a little about evaluating the progress of ideas through a network, for example ideas which are any or all of these 3 factors will tend to progress further and with more strength than ideas that did not have these features.

The lifeworld can be seen as a way of talking about individuals having multiple overlapping identities which can be seen each in a different social and thus institutional context. A farmer may have a family lifeworld, where he is powerful through patriarchy, yet be under a landlord in another lifeworld, the economy. A worker may be a Christian, and thus be influenced by a priest, yet he is also a money lender and therefore forms an economic institution, and also is part of a union of workers at his company.

Integrating the lifeworld idea into memetic analysis as developed into the identification of different overlapping networks of people leads us to the methodology of observing reality and drawing diagrams similar to idea maps. Where each person can, through having multiple lifeworlds, many occurrences in different networks of idea movement. Clearly this is a potential source of new research.

Understanding change in society requires the integration of the above lifeworld-memetic-network complex with conversation trees, that is recurrent debates which sustain a belief or change people's minds put into the rubric of extensive form game theory.

Social Forces

From Marx we can simplify or compress the information of society into the idea of social forces which are made up of nodes, their belief system and the linkages between them, as well as numerous associated idea maps. Social forces are invisible yet powerful like water. The wave is not a characteristic of an individual H2O molecule just as a social force is not a characteristic of a node.

Social forces affect society in many ways and often have a hydra like quality, that is where they are blocked they will push harder elsewhere.

They suggest activity which is not necessarily coordinated but acts in the general interest of the social force. There may be influential members of the force, both historical and present day, but the essence of this is that it is not like an organisation with a command structure nor does it follow rules given from its leadership but rather evolves behaviour based on the rules that make up the members and the dynamics of the groups that it is composed of.

Idea Transference

The process of idea transference from one node to another is not necessarily a voluntary experience. A person may not like an idea but may still be persuaded by it. Whether this sort of experience leads to greater dissemination of an idea is in doubt.

We can look at idea transference analogously to the synaptic model of the brain. Each node is subject to an activation function such that high input from a single node (a very interesting and credible idea) or multiple small inputs from several nodes (the pressures of conformity) each have the same effect of sending a message from the target node to others in the network.

Nodes can be of various types, centre nodes that are connected to most other nodes, like the media, the World Bank, government. There are slave nodes, which only receive input from a master node but do not send messages to others and there are also multiples, which have many different connections into themselves from various sources. Under certain conditions particularly where there are mutually exclusive (see below) messages being sent to a multiple node, there is the possibility of confusion in the node.

As ideas are transmitted across the network they are compressed, especially successful ones. This information compression leads to signal degradation which causes ideas to change as they pass through the network. Information compression leads to a culture of experts developing who can fully understand the compressed signals. Information compression also leads to distorted communication. However, consensus is only possible with information compression so we counter Habermas.

Idea evolution

In science, ideas evolve as Popper has said, via a process of criticism that leads to better ideas superseding old ideas. The rules of a set of nodes that generate, criticise and synthesise ideas create an evolution of ideas. These rules are both written and unwritten, coming from tradition as well as created by actions of nodes while creating ideas. We can predict the trajectory of idea evolution from these rules.

Filters

Filters to ideas exist across the system and also within nodes themselves. These stop certain kinds of ideas from propagating or lead to ideas that have a lot of memetic potential but do not fit the filter criteria being adapted to fit the filter.

Effect of ideas on nodes

Ideas move around and activate nodes due to the apparent coherence of the idea with the interests of the node or node complex. Different often mutually exclusive ideas often try to hold to the same interests so there is need for research in which ideas are taken up, propagated and held to.

Memesis

When ideas reach a certain saturation point in the node network they start to generate a consensus. This means that nodes that previously did not believe start to believe. This results in truths being formed which are held for long lasting periods of time and can be a barrier to further change and progress in society.

The effect of democracy and freedom norms on progress

Free speech, free values (that is the ability of nodes to overturn old traditions in favour of new ones), free universities and also a free press leads to a greater amount of creation, adaptation and synthesis of ideas. They also lead to greater amounts of dissemination of ideas thus raising the prospect of people with the ability of creating, synthesising and adapting ideas being able to hear about new ideas and cross-fertilizing their efforts. Democracy, by which we mean free and open debate, allows criticism thus leading to participants improving the quality of ideas. Old traditions and world views which hold back progress in ideas due to the existence of a paradigm of knowledge can be overcome with a rebellious instinct among the people who create, disseminate, adapt and synthesise ideas. Essentially more ideas are created by a true democracy and thus the solution to a problem is more likely to be found under those circumstances. Essentially the mechanism is one of distributed problem solving arising from the innate limitation of the human mind to deal with large and complex problems. By many people attacking a problem and its parts then solutions can be found that would not occur under a situation of just a few people dealing with problems.

Democracy as it has evolved in many countries has adopted a problematic strategy. Promises are made which raise the amount of nodes that align themselves with a particular social force which causes a bubble in the centre of gravity. This bubble bursts in parts of the system leading to disenchantment with democracy. The challenge for future leaders is to develop new ideas that will lead to a resolution of the desires of nodes.

Idea maps

Ideas are linked to one another forming structures called idea maps. Anthropology is linked to Sociology, though ideas in the former, like heterogeneity differ from the homogeneity of the latter. Thus tensions exist within idea maps, which can be understood and even exploited. The fact that idea maps can be so big means that though they travel in packets across nodes and are reassembled by nodes there is often the chance that these tensions will not be spotted until the idea map has become internalised (that is accepted) by many nodes. This process of sending packets of ideas which are later linked together, similar to the internet, leads to idea evolution (creation, adaptation and synthesis).

Social forces form and influence idea maps, creating new linkages between ideas over time. Objectives of clever people often lead to idea maps being strategically used.

From Baudrillard we see that ideas and relationships from ideas can be the product of the interaction of more than one person. Thus the therapist takes their legitimacy from the patient as Baudrillard puts it. The state shores up its legitimacy from the people. Opinion polls pose the question of policy to the voter but notably no new idea is created, only an existing framework. The idea of the simulacrum is interpreted by us as the existence of ideas that are not linked to the real. These ideas are short circuits of the real, that is where feedback occurs to create the idea. These ideas come from simulation. This is taken to be the production of ideas that has no link to anything real. Of course our definition of the real departs from Baudrillard who sees the whole of America to be a dream. Our real is that which can be observed, the rest is hypothesis, to see the eclipsed sun one must posit from the arc that it is roughly circular. Is a hypothesis real. If it is true it is. The problem with Baudrillard's analysis is simply that he does not define his real but gives a political gasp of the left. Ideas do lose their basis in the real since we see that they undergo dynamics given by the sociology of knowledge. An unwritten art nevertheless. Can a production of ideas ever be brought back to the real? Without the consensus creating experiments of science there is difficulty in doing this in culture and democracy. The process of rationality in culture and democracy is an object of inquiry for this. We have specified a system of society but we have not said much about the process of rationality. Even forgiving the political language games in culture and democracy, what hope is there for finding the truth. The problem is fundamentally that of the subjectivity of the agent. The truth is hidden so it is not possible to construct a proof of what would create the truth. Our ideas on democracy create more ideas but how do you determine which idea to follow. This depends on the many visions and outcomes of different policies. The construction of the outcomes of policy is to be determined in debate and with recourse to methodology, information and model building. This has the prospect of building an intellectual class who determine the outcome of policy and therefore determine the choice of policy. This would be undemocratic. However, if it is possible, one could alleviate this by information compression and clarification of policy analysis so that these could be widely disseminated and thus discussed by an increasingly educated society. Thus education is the key to democracy.

Baudrillard's simulation and simulacra states the hypothesis that reality has become superseded by a hyperreality. A simulation. Reality is corroding through disuse. He states that culture and the media have in essence created an incredibly detailed empire we live in which is not real. Does reality ever get to the truth though? And how is it that this hyperreality has been formed? Has reality ever been real? This solipsist world view is interesting but difficult to integrate in our thought.

The production of ideas will be influenced by interests and social forces, thus leading one away from truth, possibly. This could be the mechanism that creates the hypereal. The evolution of ideas, the fact that ideas are mimetically transmitted from one person to the next and undergo changes or mutations over time is quite in line with our thinking and is a point Baudrillard makes. He suggests that this gives us the idea without the model due to excessive copying, but this is a result of the increasing movement of ideas in post-modern societies. The fact that ideas change in transmission due to higher levels of education in society is not something to be worried about. It is the source of social change. The fact that it happens quickly without much thought is problematic. This is simply part of society. The feeling Baudrillard has is one of horror at the lack of any systematic basis for ideas. This comes back to our question of the difficulty of judging between ideas to get the best idea.

Idea maps have plausible courses of evolution. The tensions in a subject may be resolved, by discrediting of ideas in the map or by resolution through changes of definition and category. From Popper or Hegel, we can say that ideas may be criticised and become better or discarded for new ideas. It is a question as to whether you can really prove that this will lead to the real, the truth.

Ideas may also become the focus of political language games. They typically involve the expression of an interest of the participants or of the expected audience of the idea as given by the writer of it. This does not necessarily lead to false ideas, since the interest and the correspondence to the real model of the world are not mutually exclusive ends. Ideas that represent an interest or use a tradition seen as antagonistic to a group may be rejected irrationally by that group.

The work of Kuhn tells us that ideas evolve through paradigm shifts though Schumpeter is an earlier proponent. Idea evolution becomes clogged in existing traditions and viewpoints that need great works to be overcome and lead to new ideas.

Ideas form archetypes over time, with ideas being changed incrementally from earlier ideas. This is easier to do and also gives credit to a pre-existing set of classic works in a subject. They give people a sense of history and also define an identity.

We need a way of looking at ideas that is going to tell us how they are likely to evolve. How do you start this? How do you understand creativity? Clearly the idea comes from the object of enquiry, the themes of the subject. Just as Wittgenstein broke down philosophical enquiry with his proof that all of it was simply language games which were nonsense, so the object of enquiry changes with ideas. This kind of idea, an idea that drives the direction of the subject, typically made by the great and respected scholars, is a meta-idea. You have to generate a model of meta-ideas to determine the evolution of ideas. There is a sort of patron-client relationship between meta-ideas and ideas.

Conversation trees

It is hypothesised that we can compress the information of typical conversations relating to objects of enquiry into conversation trees, that is the main paths that the conversations can go. The effect on node belief and propagation as well as the likelihood of idea evolution can be understood with this kind of analysis.

Engaging in writing out conversation trees we can apply the framework of extensive form game theory. A debate may go ahead in society where person A makes a racist comment and person B blocks further comments by apply a rebuke of "that's wrong. That's racist". Similar simple trees have been exploited by many elites and political groups as well as nation-states to deflect criticism of their activity. For example, conversation trees can be influenced by law. It is against the law to justify terrorism in the UK. This was possibly enacted because a key argument of the anti-War Left was to say that Western foreign policy was creating terrorism, which can loosely be felt to be a justification of terror, even though it is certainly not intended to be. Thus a sleight of hand allows the government to continue to pursue its policy with conversations in Britain being restricted by law from arguing compellingly for peace, paradoxically through a law that is meant to stop the justification of violent acts.

Archetypes

We suggest a hypothesis whereby ideas spread through a society through a succession of archetypes, that is frameworks for ideas that give rise to ideas that are similar. This is due to the fact that the mind creates ideas from a base of another idea. Thus ideas evolve in small steps, but there can be discontinuous jumps. An example is the 'good' archetype which gives rise to the moral high ground. From Jesus' Christianity springs Marxism by way of Liberalism. Different people have different conceptions of good, so a Muslim's good springs from adherence of an idea to Islamic teachings whereas a Liberal's good comes from adherence to commonly held conceptions in Liberal societies and writings by liberal philosophers.

Archetypes are important idealisations of ideas, in the sense that we are taking the idea map concept through time, looking for links between ideas along the axis of time. We hope that research into this area will lead to identification of possible drivers, processes and mechanisms involved in the change of ideas in history.

Adorno

Adorno argued that cultural production is the product of capitalism. We would come to argue that culture is determined by the interaction of many agents in a system where messages are sent to one another. The fact that a consensus occurs that is in line with the interests of capitalists is not necessarily the product of bourgeois interaction in the system but rather a stable state that occurs. It is not to say natural, just a recurrent feature of societies, that consensus occurs and intersubjective domains become truths. Adorno also argues that culture becomes more exchange value than use value, i.e. the value of the idea in terms of what someone else will pay for it is greater than the intrinsic value of an idea, thus ideas have a tendency to become fruitless and meaningless hype. The hyperreality of Baudrillard is an example, as is much advertising. However the reaction from society to advertising and hype especially from an ever more sophisticated youth has lead the corporate world down perhaps a slightly different path. Here we see that the desire for corporations to legitimise themselves as well as their products has lead to an emphasis on corporate social responsibility, though whether this is entirely effective or any more than pleasant gestures is another question. In the corporate world and anti-capitalist social movements of the late 20th Century we see a strategic interaction and alteration of strategy in response to that.

This leads us to the question of how does value of a message affect the distribution of the messages in the system. Messages which are valuable to people will tend to be propagated by them. An example is the marketing messages of a business. These messages are valuable to the business since they raise sales, so they are propagated by them. Social movements develop due to the fact that the messages that make people want to join a social movement are valuable to the supporters of this. They may be valuable for religious or ethical reasons, or perhaps due to identity. They may be about a belief in a different vision for the world. They may place one in a different relationship with things. This expands on the idea that interests determine messages and their acceptance. If an idea is universally valuable then it is highly likely that it will spread across the entire system. However, ideas have associations with other ideas so it is inevitable that many universal ideas will be associated with a discrediting idea that limits acceptance by some members of the population.

It should be noted that the existence of social movements where ideas are spread for free and with little of no exchange value, contradicts the theory Adorno put forward about exchange value superseding use value in culture.

Our idea of archetypes should be seen as similar to the criticism Adorno made about mass culture, in that it is standardised with small changes. A person who reads a book will not buy a second copy of it but may buy another one of the same genre. This is an interesting process. A person who hears the message of a social movement may come to join other social movements of the same genre over time as they age, perhaps dropping involvement in earlier movements. The general principal is that the desires of a person are defined by their positive experiences. A positive experience with a book compels one to find another positive experience. A person who goes on a protest and finds something positive about knowing that they have an identity or perhaps feels like they are conforming to ethical rules of theirs will be more inclined to activity of the same sort. The mind seeks to reproduce positive experiences and forms habits from this. This is part of the process of identity formation. Identity is however something that is ascribed socially so this process is both from around oneself and from within in interaction with the environment.

Saussure

The sign is the linguistic unit which is composed of the signifier (the word) and the signified (the object the word refers to). The signs however do not adequately focus us on the object in question, the understanding of culture. Therefore the use of the sign as an analytical unit is obfuscating, rather like cutting an engine into small equal sized cubes rather than its component parts (the valves, the carburettor, battery, etc). We suggest idea maps and ideas themselves as alternative analytical units. Ideas are composed of signs but they are units that actually occur in society. Ideas vary between people, even the same idea will have a different conception in different minds. We suggest a hypothesis that ideas among a group of people come to be homogenised by interaction between those people. Human beings have the desire to herd. However, humans have an appreciation of newness. Thus new ideas, even if only slightly different, will spread quickly. Thus there is a dynamic between ideas coming together, synthesising, and then finding themselves dropped for new ones. The society breathes ideas.

26. The early 21st Century global circuits of trade and capital

Is the long term growth of China and the US a zero sum game? Do countries always gain from trade? A key characteristic of China-US circuits of capital is that China sells goods to the US and receives flows of foreign exchange which may then be recycled into the US through capital investment. Is this process sustainable and can an economy overtake the leader?

China's growth since the economic reforms of the 1980s has involved money creation through supporting the employment of people in State owned enterprises (SOE). The loans given to SOE are seen as non-performing, though one must ask whether this is due to over borrowing and interest compounding or because there is a fundamental problem of value generation within these institutions. China is in a bind as if it should withdraw funding support from SOEs then there will be large amounts of unemployment and knock on effects throughout the economy. Clearly as an aside the nature of ownership of a firm does not affect necessarily the value generation it is able to produce. Modern corporate capitalism involves often many short term investors in shares of companies with day to day management by a class of executives who have been selected on merit and ability by a fairly objective and rational process of interviews. Since corporate capitalism is often very good at generating value, there seems to be no issue of whether state owned enterprises in China cannot become better value generators.

A spreadsheet analysis of a process of two trading economies with asymmetric levels of trade running in opposite to the imbalance in GDP (America has $13 trillion GDP, China has $2 trillion) involving money being transmitted in a constant proportion to GDP from America to China would lead to a steady convergence (see graph below). What we see from China is that there is a diminishing rate of increase in GDP from trade, principally assuming that GDP falls in America. Clearly this is an abstract simulation of a process of movement of money between two nations and denies complexity. However the insight brought from this is that China cannot move ahead of America through trade alone, it needs domestic growth in the circuits of capital to raise its GDP above the US. Therefore the predictions of the Goldman Sachs model of China's growth are called into question. We must stress that this is just one process among many that are always occurring in economies. But simply on trade alone, China cannot grow past America.

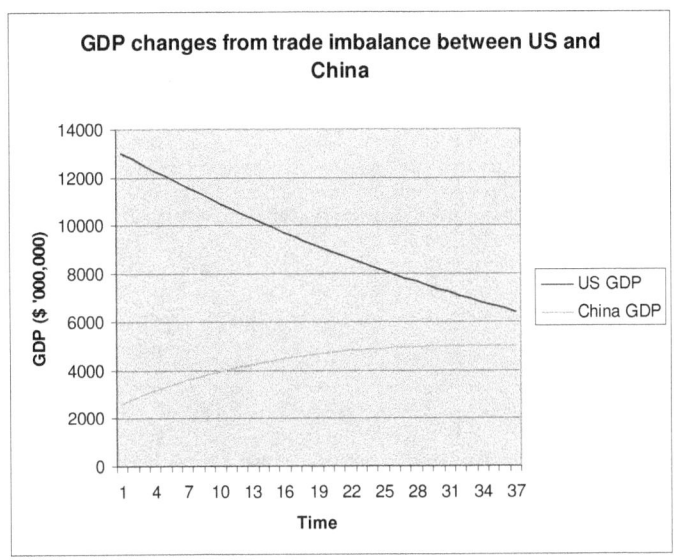

27. The Private Equity Model

Early 21st century high finance saw the evolution of a new, experimental and initially successful business model; private equity. This involves buying companies using packages of financial instruments like loans and bonds that split up the earning streams of companies. The efficiency aspect of the innovative model was to split up existing businesses and put them together with other ones to create synergies and cross market/production possibilities for income growth.

While there was an initial boom in the early development of this sector with funds and human capital moving into it at the prevailing low interest rates of the post 9/11 world economy, the underlying model came to be reconsidered. At the root was the determination of where exactly the exorbitant returns were coming from. Moving beyond the obfuscation of the complex financial instruments used to fund buyouts of public firms and putting them into less scrutinised private hands we hypothesise that the salient difference between private equity and other capitalist models is in fact that there is far higher levels of debt to shareholder capital. Since the rate of return on capital is higher at higher levels of leverage given low interest rates on debt, the illusion of a highly profitable industry is created. Small changes in profit to the business that is bought produced by private equity reassembly of firms in their portfolio lead to large changes on return on capital. The risks of this approach became apparent when interest rates rose in the 2007 credit crisis leading to a flight to low leverage, consistent profitability rather than rate of return on capital. The process of private equity raising the amount of leverage on firms leads to risks to the liquidity of business within the economy which leads to instability given variation in macroeconomic variables.

We suggest that business strategy must be expanded to consider the macro effects of the implementation of such strategy on the system, through simulation of outcomes and scenario analysis of the potential risks. Clearly should government be the only party in such analysis then there is the potential for asymmetries of information between industry and government to produce ineffective analysis. However, as new trends and changes in the structure of the economy are observed, economists could be a satisfactory alternative to government, by engaging with the private sector to gather information on the actual structure of the economy and then using their analytical skills to debate the sustainability of different structures and processes. This would lead to greater intertemporal transparency of business, in other words business would be better understood by the society at large, not just in terms of its existing realities but in terms of the future potential reality. Investors would thus be able to allocate capital more effectively across different business models and more stable business models would demand a higher premium, thus drawing firms towards a more effective long term growth strategy, which, given that the economy is partly the sum of all firms within it, would have a strengthening of long term growth.

28. Extensive form game theory applied to poverty and crime

Extensive form game theory is a mathematical form which deals with strategic interactions along an axis of time. I choose to move my knight to attack your pawn, you sacrifice your pawn but this allows your queen to move closer to the king. This results in me engaging in a different path and thus you can take my bishop. Any interaction can be considered. However who are the players? Are they truly restricted to humans with free will? We consider the conceptualisation of society or one's environment as a strategic player in human interaction. Just as the economist would say that the firm makes its decisions in a response to the market, so we suggest thinking of the poor individual as engaging in a strategic reaction with their environment as a player in the game, expressible through extensive form game theory.

Discussion with the disillusioned poor person may bring to light a feeling they have that the world is against them, that it seems hopeless, they have nothing to look forward to, perhaps a general disrespect for tools of society like the police and that it seems they just can't seem to get any further. The human propensity for anthropomorphism is idea that objects in the world have a human quality. Humans are based on relations with other humans, it is integral to our brains we assert, and so our relationship to our environment can lead to a consistency in the ascription of 'a soul' to society. Humans show great loyalty, at times, to royalty and their nation-state, their culture. No where is the anthropomorphic nature of the mind more clear in the embodiment of a nation-state as an actual person, whether royalty or president.

As a poor person interacts with society they are hypothesised to generate a relationship with it as an idea map in their own mind. These idea maps are transmitted between different members of poor communities. This idea map is more along the lines of a conversation tree in that it is a strategic extensive form interaction. One can choose to get welfare payments, sell drugs or get a job. The lack of success at getting a job that fulfils the poor person can lead to other options being revised in their expected payoff. Clearly society is a conscious phenomena in that it is organised and lead, so the government structures incentives to discourage deviant behaviour.

We hypothesise that the environment of the poor has a tendency to lead to many no-win options in the extensive form game theoretical payoff tree of the poor person. This causes frustration leading to a tendency to underachieve, apathy, violence, crime, breakdown of family and other social institutions. For example, if one has a low income then one may be in possession of a second hand TV. This outlet and release from ones life may be prone to breaking down. Thus one may work all day and find that the only escape one has leads to frustration when it breaks down or gives a poor picture quality. We must see that it is not the particular effect of a dodgy TV that causes crime but a multitude of processes that lead to the frustration of the poor and thus deviant and destructive outcomes. The nature of contemporary US capitalism is perhaps related to this and work to lift the Americans out of their poor state must be undertaken in order to overcome the concomitant problems of its system. The implication for globalisation is that the US model is not completely perfect and to avoid the difficult social problems of the US there must be adequate solutions to the neglect of the poor's environment interactions from an analytical systemic rubric.

29. What makes an idea successful?

An idea is successful if it is held by large numbers of people. Assuming that an idea comes from a single source, it must overcome mutual exclusive ideas and disseminate widely throughout society. We suggest that there are strongly held idea maps in society and in its various groups which a successful idea must be coherent with at least, and for high chances of success it must be something that springs from, that is a development from the underlying idea map.

Consider corporate branding. Practitioners know that you can sell a lot of product if there is a good brand identity. Look at Coca-Cola or various goods sold to the youth. Adverts for these products have often related the good and brand with the idea of being 'cool', in other words consumption of this product will raise or maintain your social status among a youthful peer group. Skin care products often have the idea of beauty associated with them, along with a 'science bit', in other words there is a scientific causal mechanism that the product involves that gives legitimacy to the products effectiveness. This brings together two different contrasting ideas, beauty of the self and science as a cure for all problems. The point is that these are underlying ideas in society and thus advertising practitioners tend to use them to successfully raise sales. Corporate Social Responsibility is another example of linking ones brand to ones community by making the brand associated with the underlying idea map category of 'doing good'.

Determining how to make one's idea successful involves collecting data, whether informally or formally, analysing the underlying consensus idea map of the group one wishes to affect. Linking your idea as a natural result of the underlying idea map, indeed using it as a sign of what people want, is a distinguishing point in our argument.

Clearly the effect of linking needs to be considered strategically in terms of what others in the market do. So if everyone is doing exactly the same thing then there is no effect on the demand for the branded goods. Porter would suggest examining capabilities of ones firm and seeing where there is difference with competitors such that the ideas one attaches to ones brand are most powerfully fulfilled. Café Direct distinguish themselves by providing better supplier relations (through paying them higher prices) in poor coffee growing countries and achieve increased value added results. One also has to look to develop capabilities to maintain such a difference in brand idea map. One area of capabilities is to develop the understanding of underlying idea map processes.

Understanding the dynamics of the underlying society idea map is a crucial area of research since it essentially allows you to forecast trends. Consider the fact that the concept of the "holiday" does not exist in India. However looking at the pace of life in India, whether it is the 5 day cricket match, the slow cooking of tea or the 3 hour long bollywood films, one sees a definite lack of time-compression in lifeworlds there. Thus the lack of stress in life leads to less of a need for a concept of a holiday when one gets a change in one's lifeworld to one where there is a very unrestrictive lifeworld in terms of time and itenary. However with sustained economic growth and the increase in time compression of lifeworlds, there is the likelihood of the memetic propagation of the lifeworld of the holiday to India's populace, especially its middle class, and thus one could forecast a travel industry developing there in the future. Here we see that lifeworld structural development can be influenced by economic transformation and goals and thus the underlying idea map of society can have new ideas implanted into it. The holiday in the UK is linked to the image of the beach and the scantily clad sunbathers under the sun and by the sea, among other ideas. It would be interesting to see what India's holiday idea would link to, clearly something that is prized as somewhere different to a hot country.

30. Progressive social movements in the UK

We look at idea maps for an archetype in the UK's social movements which we term 'the progressives'. The archetype involves many different social groups which have a common ethos, that of the social being above the individual. In this respect all of these social movements have been often related to being 'good' morally and have often surfaced and expressed themselves in opposition to a different social force, that of the established order. All of these movements differ in their solutions, critical ideas in their maps.

The antiglobalisation movement of the late 90s and early 21st Century involved environmental protection, a contestation of wealth and living standards between the 'rich' and 'poor' nations, direct action groups, anarchist anti-state control of the population of western countries, anti-multinational firms, anti-neo-liberal post modernist socialist academics and theorists as well as many who were simply following the crowd with little commitment to any particular ideology or outcome. What should be noted is that were one to draw out an idea map for each of these elements of the movement then there are glaring contradictions; the pro-state socialist alongside the anti-state anarchist, the pro-development of the developing countries agenda alongside the anti-industrialisation of the environmentalist. The absence of a coherent ideology suggests an important point, that social movements can ally themselves to each other and engage in varying degrees of political contestation without having a coherent plan of action for policy. Unlike socialism which had from Marx onwards a strong emphasis on debates and dissemination of theoretical and empirical developments, the tendency to coherency of ideas in a movement that becomes settled and reproduced was lacking. Charles Tilly defines social movements as phenomena of the modern Western world given the production of education which effectively means that the ability for ideas to propagate throughout society to find consensus among different individuals was more likely to occur. The common underlying idea map (truth) created by national education lead to ideas that related to this consensus of truth becoming drivers for social movements.

In an attempt to explain why incoherent idea maps of different social groups could form the anti-globalisation movement, we believe that the core motivation for engagement in these different strands of progressive thought was the desire to be 'morally good'. Since the individual may have linked incoherent ideas such as environmentalism, development of the developing countries, socialism and anarchism to being a good cause there was motivation to become a member of them. Charities are among the only organisations that can obtain a workforce to some degree without paying wages, which is due to the fact that people will engage in activity that they say is good for no monetary compensation. Similarly the progressive social movements were classes as good causes and thus people became involved, attracted to them and avoided critical analysis of them. The lack of critical analysis lead perhaps to the decline of this movement since it did not bequeath a coherent basis of either action or strategy which is the key for reproduction of an institution. But the key point to realise is that the underlying consensual idea map of society involves being 'morally good', and indeed many justifications for different ideological approaches are linked to the underlying idea map by attaching to the 'morally good' idea. Democracy is linked to the government being good since it works for the people of the nation and is the common consensus of ideas according to Rawls. Laissez faire economics is argued to be in the interests of society according to mathematical models. Socialism is said to be in the interests of the working class, which form in many cases the majority of a populace. Anarchism is in the interests of the people in terms of obtaining their freedom from the state. Monarchy is argued by Hobbes to be crucial to society since it establishes order among people. The common theme from at least the 14th Century is that ideas must be linked to the 'moral good'. However they differ on whose good, an anarchist takes the individual's good to be above the nation's, while socialism sees the working class' good to be above the capitalist class.

The antiglobalisation movement formed the latest in a long run theme in the UK of Progressive politics which arguably originates out of religion, perhaps the most early of social movements, which established or at least formalised the idea of morally good as distinct from morally bad. The development of the peace movement which arose out of the ashes of the antiglobalisation group in the early 21st Century was another example of this idea of good, but in this case the arguments tended towards a 'moral high ground'. The attack on America by Muslims was seen as bad, but the attack on Muslims by America was also seen as bad. Thus the logical position one obtains that involves being neither in favour of war on either side, thus a peace movement became the cause of attraction of progressive politics. The observation of this dynamic had an effect on the US administration by their seeking to at least portray their actions as the moral high ground, though the implementation of this was curbed by possibly a lack of experience of the nature of good becoming a strategic variable in public informational-support interactions.

As a member of the antiglobalisation movement during its time, I find myself reporting that the membership entailed an identity and furthermore a completely different life world in Habermas' terminology where one experienced exciting and involving interactions. The change in the very rules, values and goals one had during a demonstration, with its dynamic of strategic interaction with law enforcement authorities, made for an escape from the mundane realities of consumer capitalism. This free holiday into a world were one's reason for being somewhere was in line with the underlying idea map of 'moral goodness' lead to a coherency not found when one engages in the other pleasures of life in the post-industrial world. This is above all the key to the development of the movement in that it produced in different groups an alternative life world, with different language, meaning of objects changing and action differing alongside a coherency of being. It redefined space as well as the mental existence, for example the march on Oxford street that lead to Oxford circus becoming a temporary prison for the demonstrators when they were cornered there by police and arrested as a group under public order legislation.

31. Nightlife

We turn our discussion to the lifeworld in Western culture of nightlife. In the UK this perhaps can be seen to begin with social institutions of the tavern, the pub. There were many kinds of developments in this into places where dance was integrated into the 'nightlife' lifeworld. Dance, as a social institution existing within a zone, a building or room, this widely found cultural phenomena was perhaps an elite institution that became widely held. 'The ball' was an attachment of the idea of dance with an elegantly designed building that brought together people of that class. The modern night club, in some cases, can be seen as an extension of this idea map, but with a liberal equality slant to it. While the life world of the nightclub in the 21st Century is a barrier of security staff who define entry, alongside a monetary transaction, which follows a mixing up of social relations within the process of the darkness mixed with light effective of consciousness as much as the intoxication of drugs and alcohol. Many people who have been to a nightclub would report a feeling of elation and satisfaction which comes perhaps from the simplifying effects of the lifeworld, allowing one to forget ones work lifeworld, and the engagement in social relationship building, the expansion of social networks, whether transient or more long lived. This may explain the popularity of the nightlife concept in Western culture, broadly a category in the underlying lifeworld idea map of 'entertainment'. The limitation of the individual to affect this idea map, even though they are the source of it, shows that memetic phenomena can be very stable.

Were one to be against 'nightlife', then the concept still remains and is reproduced, since someone who opposes 'nightlife' simply stays at hope at night and therefore ceases to be a part of this lifeworld. Clearly there is the possibility of the entire society opposing nightlife and then the concept would no longer occur, so there must be a central mechanism leading to the tendency for nightlife to be in existence. The gain for members of the nightlife world is a soothing and expelling of frustration, boredom and anger. The work lifeworld, the engagement in employment, leads to these needs being created, thus the stress of modern life leads to a symbiotic relationship with nightlife as a lifeworld, where nightlife supports and maintains the lifeworld of work by allowing a controlled dispersion of stress and frustration. As a result of the capitalist system of exploitation and alienation, nightlife becomes a set part of the social structure and time-geography.

We can see a similar analysis with the maintenance and stability of the social structure of the work lifeworld. This is due to the fact that any who oppose 'work' can only respond by not being part of the world of work, thus they are unemployed and therefore exist outside this lifeworld and do not affect it. Thus the work lifeworld remains and is reproduced as a system of domination. This basic fact has not been understood by Giddens in his Structuration theory. He maintains a seemingly contradictory stance that social agents are able to change their social systems of domination, yet are simultaneously part of them. What is clearly our distinction with Structuration theory is that as soon as one opposes a stable social structure, whether dominating or benign, one is often excluded from it, whether by design or accident. The absence of an 'author' to many social institutions and collectivities leads to a difficulty in altering them by individual parties.

What we can understand from this analysis is that the lifeworld is an experience in many cases, thus it reproduces itself via a spectacle where audience is actor, with varying people involved in it. There are rules and patterns of behaviour but the stability of the concept is established without formal discussion within society or theoretical work as to it. Thus we can see that social institutions can arise out of history rather than having the individual author. This is a key point in our understanding of the macro-micro homogeneity-heterogeneity social-individual division. The individual cannot change nightlife, even though they are the constituents of it. While they may not desire to change it because it gives a well trodden path to go down with well understood expectations, this leads us into a development of the analytical work of the nature of the structure that leads poverty into crime and tension. The argument that social theory has presented that domination in a social structure cannot coexist with free will can be understood by application of the principal of nightlife, which is a common experience of many of our readers, that the individual often chooses the well trodden path and can in many ways be seen as engaged in a non-deliberative engagement and reproduction of social institutions such as nightlife. We put the question of whether the many other alternative lifeworlds of the modern society are not also similarly one of being part of something which one cannot change in its core idea map and life world existence.

32. On the salient characteristics of the underlying idea map of society

Different societies have varying idea maps, we take that as an assumption that is evident from the literature. But is there a structure that determines or at least drives a process that leads to a tendency to skew the idea map in one or other direction of change?

Clearly since the society is formed of humans then the underlying idea map, the common truths, will be related to the human as an individual. We should reduce this to common ideas in idea maps will be formed in relation to the individual. As a human one has the desire for survival, so we can deduce that a common category of ideas will be linked to the concept of a threat. So x is a threat or y is a threat. It may be couched in more dense terms, such as x is linked to a process which will (between the lines) be considered a threat at some point in the future. The media in the West links crime with black people, or immigration with modern slavery (i.e. people trafficking), precisely to create this commonly interpreted linkage to the concept of threat.

There is also the commonly held concept of 'good', which must be seen in an abstract form that is ascribed by the individual. Charity is closely linked to the concept of 'good', and people alter their reaction to charities compared to organisations that have been attached to the idea of 'threat', such as the multinational corporation idea in the anti-capitalist movement. Clearly the concept of good and threat are subject to their own historic dynamic in terms of their definition.

Just taking these two conceptual categories; good and threat, we can see that many basic strategies in information politics can be created simply by adjusting idea maps to link different political objectives to either good or threat.

Idea map coherence between environmentalism and Christianity

Consumerism   Covetousness
     /   /
Carbon Emissions   God's Judgement
     /   /
Global Warming   Hell

Consider the environmental movement. The idea map which has 'popped' into a system wide belief is one of the linking of the threat to the planet with carbon emissions. It is not necessarily true that the world will end if there are carbon emissions, however a promotion as good of ideas of non-covetousness has reappeared in Western society (this was last seen in the Christian inspired linking of covetousness with going to Hell, a similar idea to global warming, especially in its irreversibility) because of the linking of carbon emissions and a threat to the survival of the human race. What we see here is a dynamic between linking an idea to 'threat' and the formation of what is 'good'. Good things are what reduce the risk of the threat from manifestation.

Was good created out of threat? Consider religion. If one takes the Old Testament God to be valid, then one sees the narrative of numerous nations being punished for not being 'good', thus taking the narrative as real, then one can suggest that numerous social groups that are at the roots of Western society were possibly inspired into doing good as defined by the religious texts to avoid the threat of God (i.e. through fear of God).

Good is often held to be also about the abnegation of the self, to consider others more than oneself where this helps them and to consider oneself more than others where this involves judgement. Thus we avoid taking too reductionist and generalising a view on our above analysis and hypothesis.

Good in Western society after the Renaissance came to hold an attachment with Liberalism. The linking of the idea of contained set of rights which each individual within a nation-state is thought to have necessarily with their existence; equality of opportunity (Rawls), property rights, rights to engage in the political process, rights to do whatever one wants where this does not reduce the rights of others (Mill). Liberalism, as most idea maps that are considered part of the underlying idea map, came to encompass many different ideas, for example Montesquieu separation of powers, modern ideas of duties coming with rights, the propagation of the democratic structure across the world under the Bush administration of the 21st Century, The Washington Consensus on Development for the poor countries and the state policy of privatisation of industry.

We may ask today, why does Liberalism seem so entrenched with the idea of good? Historically it is Liberalism that has been at the heart of material changes for much of humanity, for example, the end of slavery, the French and American revolutions. Clearly for an idea to become considered good, the idea must be linked to popular changes. We take the view that an idea is not inherently of a certain quality, but rather it is the linking of it to different things that gives it a quality. Were we to simply say, Liberalism is good obviously, then we would be part of one of the processes (the mimetic process) which we seek to cast light on. In terms of a society that sees progress as good, that is change of benefit, Liberalism seems a beneficial change as compared to previous belief systems. The idea of progress is perhaps something that in Western society, comes from the gradual change of capitalism over the last five centuries. So looking at the difference between old religious-feudal systems of the human condition and liberalism, one finds that more people gain from the change to equality of political power as an ideal (democracy) than from believing that they are part of a stable natural hierarchy ordained by God (religious feudalism). Clearly there are prominent thinkers providing better arguments for the need for a sovereign, such as Hobbes, who links the welfare of the individual to the power of the sovereign, by suggesting that a decline from order would result without a powerful King ruling which would lead to civil war thus hurting the individual. Here, perhaps, the idea of the concentration of power of the nation-state leads to the King being overthrown to be replaced by the King of the revolution. Thus it may be argued that Liberalism brings forward some of the ideas of the old feudal-monarchic state thus an archetype forms, one of the centralisation of power and the singularity of the leader, the key decision maker. A criticism we have of Liberalism is that how can it be considered good when it involves keeping the key structure of the old monarchy, that of a cabal of elites who are most involved in decision making. The fact that these elites have to justify their ideas to society does not make much difference as they will often be applying their own vision for society rather than one that society itself has generated. The idea of a mandate handed down by the people is not too different from a mandate handed down by God, the two are similarly immaterial and silent in this world. Thus we see that Liberalism has a fault we have sought to address in our argument for direct democracy.

The analogue of the political leader in the economy is the capitalist. Yet this has in some parts dispersed so that the idea of the leader is there in the structure of the firm, yet the owner of the firm is in a sense non-existence or at least transient in public limited companies due to the fact that the shares of these companies are traded constantly by investors with diversified portfolios. Clearly these investors all want the same thing, an increase in their asset's value, so an external silent stimulus stops any change from the goal of profit as an ethos and meaning of the firm, yet the fact is that the investors rarely have to do anything to discipline the firm's managers, the structure of the firm and economy is such that the snake moves on even when its head is cut off. This is closely related to our discussion on 'nightlife' as a structure or lifeworld that one cannot actually change much, it exists as a part of society, a strategic path of experiences that is habitually engaged with, and also our discussion on poverty structures (composed of a number of lifeworlds that are accessible to the poor) that have a tendency to lead to crime, which also cannot be changed by the individual inhabitant.

What we see then is that an inherent perfect good of Liberalism, in the sense that it is the end of history, the natural stage that all societies will become drawn to, is naïve and misleading. Liberalism contains ideas that are not huge changes from earlier illiberal ideas. It caught the winds of a social trend and was in the interests of the growing property owning and value adding classes (capitalists and other rich people). The coincidence of interests between the common man seeking some meaning and empowerment and the rich who were not part of the political elite, lead to stimulus to the acceptance of the idea of liberalism, which is what gave rise to its revolutionary power. Yet when an old order is replaced, there is often the fundamental problem of freedom (getting your freedom is easy, the hard part is knowing what to do with it) which leads to indecision and the creation of an archetype, that is in some sense a regress to the old forms with new ideas. What we talk of here is the notion of the sovereign, which is where democracy stopped being good by taking a representative relation to the public. It is as little in the interests of the public to be ruled by hereditary Kings as it is for the public to be ruled by the winner of an election, which is little more than a social memetic system which often degenerates to strategic buzz word slogan conflicts and personal image. The amount of political analysis devoted to this area of presentation and the paucity of development of coherent useful strategies to improve the nation makes this fact all the more pertinent.

The reply a liberal fundamentalist may give is that the election leads to the government becoming in line with society's interests. We need to discuss the nature of interests, that is the stimulus of a social group to go down various strategic paths. In most cases this is where the payoff for going down a specific path is considered more beneficial than others. Interests manifest from the underlying idea map in terms of causality. If x brings good things for z then z's interest will be for x. If y brings bad things for z then z's interest will be against y. Such an idea map does not need to be true, for example it may not be a measurable outcome perhaps because this will happen in the far future. People may not judge it to be as important as their vital interest in another area. The idea map may not be coherent, in which case the interest aligned government may not be able to ever deliver completely, as in the case of low taxes alongside high levels of free health care. The idea map may be simple, perhaps generated by a set of simplistic journalists, focusing on heterogeneity to determine the generality, or some similarly incoherent methodology for social comment. The journalists are determined by government and government is determined by the journalists. Thus one could perhaps see the grave problems of untenable democracy. We have given one answer to this particularly problematic feedback issue in our theory of the Islamic state, or moral nation.

A key reason why Liberalism is immune from criticism is that it has replaced what was considered Holy in the Western world. In other words it occupies position of a religion and criticism of it is seen as blasphemy (perhaps because archetypes inherit old associations). The naivety of this is clear since liberalism can only progress (progress being its original justification) through critical thought on it, in ideal and in implementation. That said, in the Western world Liberalism is strongly placed in the underlying idea map and any new ideas to be imposed on this culture would need some linking to Liberalism to be successful.

33. Defining integration of Muslims into the UK.

A process involving idea map propagation is through feedback of it between various groups or perhaps various network configurations. As two groups form through a grand narrative, there is an idea of the image of each group propagated among members of these groups. In the absence of links between these groups, in other words a linking of lifeworlds, there is the tendency for these idea maps to follow the dynamic within the group and not be based on empirical verification. Thus the idea map of imperialism which was reproduced as racism in the 20th Century West made an idea map of out groups linking various negative ideas to the identification of out-groups. A modern theme employed in anti-Islamic Western policy is to suggest that there is a problem with the integration of Muslims in Western society. There has been a paucity of real debate on what this really means, making it seem like the usual business of proto-genocidal Western rhetoric to make Western imperialism less contested. However it is interesting to discuss the whole idea of integration and the reaction to this policy (if one can call it a real policy since it has not been backed up by any measures or concrete proposals) from Muslims as a starting point for some interesting social analysis.

For example, a common Muslim rebuke to the command by the state is that assimilation, an idea with many imperialist notions, is not accepted. This is an interesting blocking strategy in the debate, since it shows that the social group under attack (Muslims) replies to the command by redefining integration as being assimilation, a negative or evil idea with links to colonial interference in ones culture. Thus Muslims do not change, therefore the whole policy of integration, based as it is entirely in news headline narrative, becomes dulled and ineffective, at least in terms of achieving the undefined idea of integration.

Why do Muslims feel threatened by the idea of integration, even though the idea is as the air; empty, vapid as liberty and in denial of basic policy methodology (which is to do something that achieves a purpose)? The implications of integration are to lose one's religion, lose ones identity and potentially lose one's place in heaven. As a social group, an integrated Islam would seem to engage in a trend of slowly withering away until there is nothing vital or distinguishing about it. This is a further problem of the vapidity of integration as a concept, since it leads Muslims to feel threatened by their own imagination about what integration entails.

The political endorsement of the idea map of "Muslims – not integrated into British society", further feels as if the subtext is really that Muslims are not part of British society. This political excommunication is deeply rooted in a theme of Western Europe, that of excluding a section of society; Jews, the working class, the poor, criminals, the insane, women, people fleeing torture and war (asylum seekers), single mothers. The result therefore of suggesting that Muslims are not integrated into society is something that actually has the effect of excluding Muslims from British society. The paradoxes and madness of civilisation is evident.

We can hazard a guess at what integration means in terms of our analytical toolkit. This is that society is composed of many lifeworlds when one considers the structures that make up the consciousness of the people. These lifeworlds overlap and interact, a child may have a peer group lifeworld when they play with their friends and have another one when they are at school, where there is an authority above them of teachers. The teacher who is less able to control the classroom results in the peer group play lifeworld being born as disruption to the lesson. Integration could mean linking lifeworlds together, not necessarily to produce disruptive chaos as our example, but rather to create a harmonious society. But lifeworlds entail different rules, viewpoints, psychological frames. So a simple bringing together of British people with UK Muslims will not necessarily work on its own. Making it law that British people had to visit a Mosque periodically and get to know Muslims would be an example of linking together lifeworlds. The expansion of Mosques into community centres where British people would link in to the Muslims lifeworld by obtaining something they required or needed, help in some way, education, talks and discussions, etc would be an alternative way to achieve the same outcome of linking lifeworlds. Sadly thanks to the media and government linking the idea of Muslim charities and mosques as centres of fundamentalism and terror this possibility is cut off and help for British people in need is robbed from them. Thus we see how a general incompetence bordering on self-destruction by the Western governments has cut off solutions to the problem once again.

34. The institutional determinants of trade

Consider the institutional differences (in the sense of classical political economy) between China and India. China has a large working class, this being considered a social group distinct from others in terms of their relations to production as well as self ascribed identity (agricultural workers in pre capitalist China would have considered themselves working class). India has a large middle class, since it produces many thousands of educated graduates every year.

Under free trade as was the policy post 1990s in India and China, we see that the institutional endowment of labour produced systematic effects on industrial structure. The companies that grew most under free trade were those that had an ample supply of labour that matched the work lifeworld that those companies offered. India's middle class service sector, for example IT, IT related industries, banking and other services, grew substantially during the liberalisation period, while conventional manufacturing was not as successful as China. China on the other hand developed strong capabilities in manufacturing with its large supply of working class labour and working class identity labour (as in agricultural workers who migrated to the industrial zones).

Thus we see that the Heckscher-Ohlin model, which suggests that endowments of resources determine costs, thus comparative advantage and therefore the pattern of production for trade, can be used as an analytical justification for this outcome. We do not agree with the methodology of the Heckscher-Ohlin model but we are able to conceive real processes leading to similar results to this.

Essentially the decision for investment in a specific sector depends on the 'beliefworld' of the entrepreneur or board of directors. This is essentially an idea map that is circulated among a class that relates to a certain decision and also involves action external to the class and also internally to reproduce, legitimise and reinforce itself. It can be seen as a lifeworld and idea map synthesised together.

The beliefworld of the entrepreneurs who invested in China and India were ideas about what could reasonably work as a business in these countries. The institutional structure, in other words the pool of skills available, lead to the beliefworld of entrepreneurs investing in China and India to be different and thus there was differing sectoral investment in them. This would be considered the 'decision maker model' hypothesis of determinants of free trade.

On the other hand one can suggest that the 'production process model' hypothesis of trade, which is where comparative advantage and thus the sectoral composition of trade depends on either / both relative cost of inputs and absolute supply, which we suggest is related to institutional structure.

Testing which of these hypothesis' is most convincing as an explanation for the outcome of free trade is an interesting lead for future research.

35. An Accumulation model

We consider a sink and a source in a dynamic fluid system. The fluid here is money and we assume that the sink is able to retain some of the fluid that passes through it. The source is the state's injection of money into the system. If the sink is the sole recipient of the money then there is an endless amount of accumulation. The retention of the fluid increases, thus we see the process of accumulation.

Consider now a simple vector which holds the values of money accumulated by each different node. The nodes can be ordered as in contemporary capitalism in a hierarchy of capitalist and working classes. As money is injected into the system, perhaps through open market operations by a central bank, whereby the banking system has an increase in money which it then lends on the basis of collateral and business plan feasibility, then capitalists will be able to increase their capital investment and marketing investment (in other words together, the value adding process) and so money will flow from the working class to the capitalist in exchange for products. Money also flows to the working class in the form of wages. This occurs at different times in each node's case so that the system does not seize up with one individual or class holding all the money. Personal debt also allows this to occur. The marketing investment alters the idea map of society to motivate people to buy products of those firms engaging in the investment.

If a party engages in consistent consumption of a product, for example defence expenditure by a government or middle class luxury good consumption, then the economy will adapt to provide for these classes of consumption, subject to there being the capabilities or the potential capabilities in this economy. Thus the economic structure of the society is dependent on the idea map of the society, in that a society may see that defence as a role of the state or that being middle class involves luxury consumption.

In a society like the US where major sections of society are not linked into capitalism in a way that allows them to extract much of a surplus above their reproduction requirements for themselves and their families, then such a system has an inherent susceptibility to crisis. The long run increase in asset prices taken as a given leads to firms requiring a higher rate of profit increase to account for ever larger amounts of debt taken on to fund operations. As a result there is a skewed bias towards middle class consumption products and therefore the poor do not find much choice or opportunity to enhance their lifeworld. As a result there is a move towards a service sector whereby middle class people consume time from the poor who are brought into a system of domination which is the service sector. The result is that society cannot grow further for long periods of time in this hierarchy of value adding. The problematic of middle class consumption leading to balance of trade deficits in America is evident. To finance this the US tries to attract foreign investment into its financial assets which inflates their value and produces an engorged financial sector and therefore greater inequality. This brought about the internet bubble and the following house price bubble. Thus we see that the US model of capitalism leads to crisis and inequality.

On the other hand were the profits of big firms recycled into income for the poor then there would be increases in market size, a flattened hierarchy of value leads to enhanced rates of growth. Thus we suggest a change in the institutional structure of society whereby all members are equal shareholders of all big firms of that society. Thus the sinks in the system become connected to the nation and therefore there is a longer growth period for the economy. Without the hierarchy of different social groups there is also less inflationary pressure from wage increases cascading across the system to maintain the relative status of different classes. Thus with the 'flat' economy there are also fewer inflationary dangers to growth. The problem is that accumulation is heterogeneous in all circumstances and to homogenize the income and wealth structure leads to a potential problem of reduction in the incentive structure to work. Thus unless this problem is solved, capitalism can never be consider to be a sustainable and good system. Clearly a socialist economy based on common shareholder ownership of the means of production of the majority of large firms in the economy would be a solution, given that it could retain a certain level of equality in terms of income and wealth.

We can present this argument as the comparison of the two cycles of money; the socialist shareholder hybrid model of common ownership and the US capitalist model.

In a society where everyone owns equal shares of the firms the cycle of money is wages being spent on consumption which gives the income of firms which is recycled as wages and profit (since everyone has equal shares of dividends), thus society is in a state of stability with injections into money flow by government to keep growth.

In the US model there is a much more chaotic cycle which tends towards crises because of its inequality. Wages here lead to consumption which determines the income of firms, which is recycled as wages, but instead profits go to shareholders, who are the class that has accumulated holdings over time historically. Thus the system leads to an ever increasing income inequality. Profits saved in the banks are invested, and loaned out subject to bank's confidence about the economic outlook and the total value of assets held by borrowers. Thus there is a tendency for assets to increase in price as more money flows into them during a boom. Clearly this leads to development of value adding capabilities in firms who borrow. But the demand side of the system is not able to increase automatically, since a major section of the society simply does not have enough money to buy all the products. Clearly the US in the late 20th and early 21st Century thought it had developed an answer to this, in the form of personal debt to finance consumption, rising asset prices fuelled by debt that was in part funded across the world's financial system. The sale of assets contributed significantly to the economic growth of the US. But clearly as sales of assets occur at higher prices, and a given mark-up return is sought by seller of assets, then there is the tendency for asset prices to lose their relationship with incomes and thus the problem of affordability occurred. Asset valuation is necessarily related to the income of the users of it, since this determines the rate of return on an asset as an income stream. The problem with debt is that it leads to money flowing to those who already have money, in effect acting as a sink which reduces the market size. Thus market size shrinks under personal debt and rising asset prices, thereby cutting off the very thing that supports asset price inflation - disposable income. The realisation that equality or the greater level of equality leads to a longer period of growth is evident from the fact that with larger market size, in other words the potential demand for products, there is greater support for firms sales strategies, and market size is determined by a level of equality of income.

36. The limitations to growth in an unequal society

Consider a money flow tree-network, where there is a single capitalist with $10, two middle class employees of the capitalist who each $5 each and 4 service sector workers who sell services to the middle class for $2 each. This simple tree has a result of leading to stagnation, since the service sector workers cannot buy goods from the middle class. The feedback does not occur, in other words the celebrated circular flow of income does not work in all cases. Thus there is a limitation to growth in an unequal society. This model can be seen to be similar to the structure of production in terms of international trade. US products are expensive so it has the income to buy from other countries but unless wages rise in the poor industrial countries such as China, there cannot be a circular flow. The problem can be seen to be caused by the indivisible unit constraint on demand. A unit of the middle class good is $5 whereas the income of the poor is $2, thus in this simple structure we see that the cost of a single unit of the good limits market size. We call this the Unit Minimum Problem. To put it in more visible terms, say a rich person produces a $50 camera each period while a poor person produces a $2 box of matches each period, then the poor person can never afford to buy the camera from the rich person because they only have $2 from selling their box of matches, though the rich person can afford to buy matches, admittedly we assume that there will be a satisficing point where the rich will not want to buy endless boxes of matches.

Society has produced a solution to this, namely debt and savings. However this is not an ahistorical phenomena, that is the very idea of a loan with interest payments above principal repayments does not necessarily have to be the only form of movement of money from rich to poor. The existence of Islamic contracts, where there are novel methods of moving money from those who have to those who have not, shows this to be the case.

Clearly we can see from the above tree formation of money flow that debt can relieve the problem of stagnation for a time, since money from the richer sections of society who save can be transferred to the poor to allow them to repay over time the cost of products which are too high a value for them to afford in one period. Thus we can get a handle on the basic problem in modern capitalism, that debt is necessary for the functioning of it in its unequal state yet debt is also the cause of the crash later on.

Consider an unequal society in terms of income as an initial condition but with equal levels of spending throughout the society, in other words everyone spent an equal amount of their income on everyone else. This does not necessarily have to be in terms of capitalist-consumer production-demand relations but could be achieved through state redistributions or contracts that were created from norms in society. This eventually leads to a state of equality in spreadsheet simulation. The simulation we carried out involved an initial conditions vector which contains each level of initial income of each person in society. This is multiplied by a transformation matrix each element of which contains the percentage of income which is transferred to each other node. Where each element is equal except for the diagonal of the matrix (which is zero if there is no saving) then the system tends towards equality over time.

A further and very simple spreadsheet simulation involves looking at a comparison of an unequal society, where national income is distributed between a few people equally, and an unequal society where national income is distributed between everyone equally. Consider an income divided by 20 people in the former case and one divided by 80 people in the latter case. An increase in income is assumed to be distributed equally between only these people (the 20 or the 80 in each case respectively). Thus the rate of increase in income is higher in the case of 20 people being 'plugged into' the capitalist system, so there is widening income inequality in such cases of 'pure' American capitalism.

Plotting the variation of income distributed equally between various numbers of people gives us the curve shown in the graph "Market size as a function of income distribution". Assuming that the Unit Minimum Problem does not occur, i.e. that the cost of a unit of a good is $1, then we can see that market size (in other words potential demand) increases as a power series $Y/(n^{-1})$ with the increase in the number of people sharing in the pie of national income.

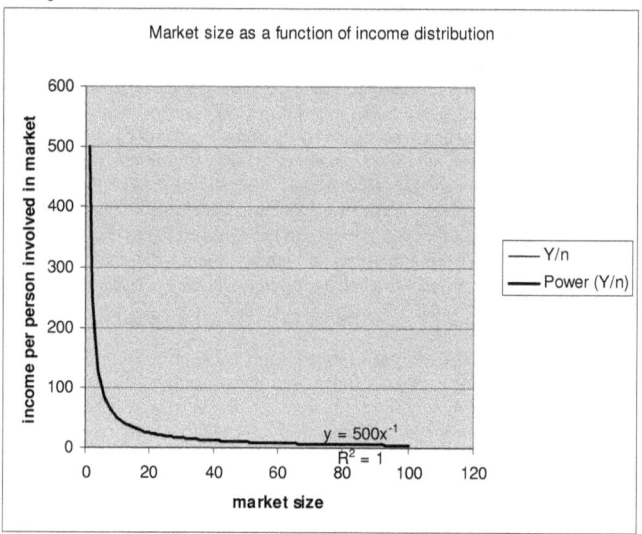

We argued in an earlier essay that raising the size of the worldwide market through measures to end poverty can lead to a higher level of world GDP due to market size being increased by a significant factor. This graph shows the mechanics of the argument for this, in other words we need to enhance the number of people getting plugged into the system or at least have a steady rate of increase in the number of people receiving a share of the world income pie, in order to sustain long term growth and indeed raise world levels of GDP growth by a significant amount.

In conclusion

We hope you have enjoyed these essays. Our goal is to develop knowledge and thus develop humanity. Focusing knowledge on real concerns of humanity, getting past the conventional wisdom and prison structures of the Liberal Reality of the developed world, we see that we can work towards progress in analytical structures that not only tell us about others but also about who we are. Life is a search for meaning and structure. Society is the answer to Life.

The issue remains to be proved whether the outcome of progression and application of the methods employed in this set of essays leads to the Truth. The reductionist social scientist may criticise that the necessary subjectivity of the approach leads to confusion and multiple arguments that overlap and cannot be brought into coherence. While logic dictates that this must occur for validity, we may reply that the entire idea that subjects should be concerned with developing a common voice is due to a social desire for academics to be more powerful. Yet as academics deviate from pluralist approaches they often deviate from the Truth. The history of humanity is littered with one common fact, if there's one thing you can depend on, it's that people will always be wrong. We realise that the enhancement of the subjectivity of analysis and thus the freedom to write as one feels and thinks leads to a proliferation of ideas, yet as Durkheim writes simple narrative of the cause of suicide, so Shakespeare writes a more complex and developed version in Romeo and Juliet. Social science is part aesthetic, whether it is in reproducing liberal ideology at its best, or producing answers to questions that we have. In ignoring the aesthetics of an argument we miss out on experiencing a key driver of the dynamic of society and therefore hold ourselves away from part of the very thing we seek to understand. Academics need to be coherent with society, the most important way to judge an analysis is to see its coherence with the object it is studying and discussing.

Furthermore we can see that the human propensity to achieve consensus, coherence of viewpoints and common messages and beliefs shown by the very existence of social objects of analysis such as institutions, ideologies, religions, political economic systems, leads one to have a hope that we can unbind the fires of academia to give light upon light to the whole world by contesting long held ideas with an explosion of new ideas. While one may say that this will lead to it being harder to identify the truth from lies, we may counter that given that we do not originally know the target, firing more shots will lead us to have a higher chance of hitting it. We may never know whether we have hit the target of truth, yet in debate, some ideas come to the fore due to the very fact that they reveal with clarity in terms of how we can look at the world, consider Einstein's thought experiments, necessarily subjective in their identification and creation, though importantly logical and reasoned in derivation of the implications of them. The result of such a debate will be that the most persuasive of ideas will percolate to the top. However, we must admit from our preceding points on memetic systems that persuasion does not necessarily have a link to the truth. It is really the biggest contemporary problem in social organisation and social science. The fact that we cannot look at empirical evidence to support claims when the society is subject to multiple processes interacting and new processes occur at various points in time means that a full determination of society is impossible. However, we can generate arguments that have their method in analysis of actual processes and social constituents which we can all see in society. We can model real processes using tools that involve looking at their dynamics though these tools must accurately represent the main features of the reality of society. Thus a dynamic optimization of household expenditure will not be privileged due to the fact that the process of dynamic optimization does not occur in reality nor can it be seen as a short cut to something that does occur. Instead we can look at a spreadsheet simulation of accumulation of a household's expenditure subject to various scenarios and then put these various simulations together to observe dynamics *in vitro*. Comparison with the empirical reality both casual (common sense) and analytical can then optimise our models and prescriptions. We can do thought experiments whereby we see if a system may tend towards stability or it may waste away or be subject to crises for example. As long as we keep the focal point of the analysis on making tools of benefit to society in terms of its self generated aims, then we are hopeful as to the efficacy of the rigour of debate.

Another confusion that may face the reader is identification of our thesis, or core argument. This must be clarified as the creation of clarifying analytical tools which can be applied in many areas of understanding social dynamics and structure in areas of society where ideas are at the core. Analysis of culture has been involving narrative and abstract models in the literature yet we see that clear observation of the reality of culture through systematic, clarifying analysis of experience can lead to considered exposition and elucidation of the social reality. We believe that some of social sciences most intractable problems can have more said about them from our tools.

Consider the contradiction between free will and an oppressive social structure. While Marxists have said that ideological chains stop classes from successful contestation of an oppressive social structure, we believe that we can look more deeply at conversation trees that produce the outcome and are essential to maintenance and reproduction of an ideological superstructure.

We believe that an extensive game theoretical analysis of the poor's life histories and their counterfactuals would lead to a broader and possibly more successful approach in dealing with poverty and crime. As an aside, we consider that the structure of poverty leads to a constant stream of events that induce frustration and fear that lead to violence, potential mental illness and crime. Marx sought to channel that stream of emotion into contestation of the allocation and control of wealth, technology and resources. Modern day de jure meritocracy seeks to bring people out of poverty as long as it is something they choose to work hard at, yet the nature of the structure of poverty in developed countries, even those with welfare states, leads to this escape route from poverty being blocked. The reason America looks for external enemies is possibly due to the presence of poverty in the US and the potential of contestation that such social disparity can create. Thus in order to solve Muslim-West relations, an understanding of poverty and crime must be considered and solved in developed countries.

www.ingramcontent.com/pod-product-compliance
Lightning Source LLC
Chambersburg PA
CBHW072230170526
45158CB00002BA/831